VALERIA SAVENKO

BURN IN

THE ULTIMATE GUIDE

TO BURN OUT

PREVENTION AND RECOVERY

Unlocking the Secrets
to Work-Life Harmony,
Personal Empowerment,
and Sustainable Well-Being

ISBN: 978-1-960136-96-1

TABLE OF CONTENTS

INTRODUCTION

Welcome to a conversation that's long overdue – a deep dive into the world of burnout, a topic that's as critical as it is misunderstood. This book isn't just a collection of insights and advice; it's an interactive guide designed to walk you through understanding, recovering from, and preventing burnout.

Here's what you'll find on the pages of this book:

1. **Unraveling the Mystery of Burnout**: We'll cut through the noise and get to the heart of what burnout really is. It's more than just feeling tired or stressed. Burnout is a complex psychological state, and understanding it requires peeling back many layers. I'll blend professional knowledge with real-life examples (minus the jargon) to give you a clear, relatable picture.

2. **Mapping the Road to Recovery**: If you're feeling burnt out, know that there's a way back. I'm here to share strategies and insights while drawing from both personal experience and my work as a therapist to help guide you on this journey. This book is about offering hope and practical steps, helping you navigate your way back to a place of balance and wellness.

3. **Championing Prevention**: Why wait to fix something if we can prevent it from breaking in the first place? Prevention is key, and this book is packed with proactive strategies. From personal habits to organisational changes, I'll show you how to create a life and work environment that's more resistant to burnout.

This book is for everyone whether you're leading a team, running your own business, or just trying to juggle life's demands. It's for those who want to understand burnout better, for leaders who aim to foster healthier workplaces, and for anyone who's ever felt the creeping shadow of burnout.

As you turn these pages, think of this book as your ally. It's here to offer you insights, be a source of comfort during tough times, and equip you with tools for a more balanced life. Together, we'll explore how to transform the challenge of burnout into an opportunity for growth and fulfilment. So, let's get started, shall we? There's a lot to cover, and I promise it'll be a journey worth taking.

PART I: UNDERSTANDING BURNOUT

Welcome to Part I of our exploration: "Understanding Burnout." Together, we will deep dive into the intricate world beneath the surface of what is often mistaken for mere workplace stress and unravel the complex tapestry of burnout, a phenomenon that remains misunderstood by many. Through the chapters that follow, I aim to illuminate the contours of burnout with clarity and depth, guiding you through the psychological underpinnings, identifiable signs and symptoms, and the root causes that sow the seeds of this condition.

In the opening chapter, "The Psychology of Burnout," I lay the groundwork for our journey. This chapter serves as a gateway into the realm of burnout, offering insights into its historical evolution and the pivotal studies that have shaped our understanding of it today. We delve into the minds of pioneers like Herbert Freudenberger and Christina Maslach, whose foundational work has provided us with a framework to grasp the multidimensional nature of burnout. Here, we explore not just the what and the why but also the how of burnout, unpacking the psychological mechanisms that underlie this complex phenomenon.

As we progress to "Signs & Symptoms," I equip you with the tools to recognise burnout, both in yourself and others. This chapter is designed to be both a mirror and a map—a mirror reflecting the often overlooked signs of burnout, and a map guiding you through the labyrinth of its manifestations. From emotional exhaustion to a sense of diminished personal accomplishment, we dissect the subtle yet profound indicators of burnout, offering clarity and understanding to those who may be navigating this challenging terrain.

Venturing further into the heart of the matter, "Root Causes" examines the myriad factors that contribute to burnout. This exploration takes us beyond the individual into the broader societal, organisational, and personal dynamics that fuel the fire of burnout. We scrutinise the structural and psychological elements at play from the imbalance of job demands and resources to the impact of personal values and societal pressures. This chapter seeks to uncover the deeper layers of burnout, challenging us to think critically about the environments we inhabit and the lives we lead.

Part I of this book is not just an academic endeavour; it is a journey of discovery and understanding. It is for the overworked employee who can't shake the feeling of exhaustion, the manager striving to support their team, and the individual seeking to understand the nuances of their own mental health. I invite you on a journey to demystify burnout, to see it not as a sign of failure but as a call to action.

As we navigate through these chapters, we lay the foundation for the transformative discussions that follow in the rest of the book. With knowledge comes power—the power to recognise, understand, and ultimately, take the first steps toward change. Welcome to *Understanding Burnout*: a guide, a companion, and a beacon of hope for those seeking to find their way back to well-being.

Defining Burnout: Historical Perspectives and Modern Understanding

In the tapestry of modern work culture, burnout emerges as a complex pattern, woven from threads of chronic stress, unmet expectations, and the relentless pace of societal progress. The concept of burnout, while seemingly contemporary, has roots deep in the history of psychological study and workplace dynamics.

The genesis of the burnout conversation can be credited to Herbert Freudenberger, a psychologist who, in the 1970s, first identified the phenomenon among volunteers at a free clinic in New York City. Freudenberger described burnout as a state of fatigue or frustration brought about by devotion to a cause, way of life, or relationship that failed to produce the expected reward. His groundbreaking work laid the foundation for a new field of inquiry, highlighting the emotional and physical toll of intense professional engagement.

Following Freudenberger's initial observations, researcher Christina Maslach expanded the scope of burnout research, introducing a multidimensional model that has become seminal in the study of workplace stress. Maslach's work, characterised by the development of the Maslach Burnout Inventory (MBI), identified three key dimensions of burnout: emotional exhaustion, depersonalisation, and reduced personal accomplishment. This model provided a structured framework for understanding and measuring burnout, facilitating a deeper exploration of its causes, manifestations, and impacts.

As the discourse around burnout evolved, so too did its recognition within the broader medical and psychological communities. The culmination of decades of research and advocacy was marked by the World Health Organisation's decision to include burnout in the 11th Revision of the International Classification of Diseases (ICD-11) in 2019. In this landmark acknowledgement, burnout was characterised as a "syndrome," conceptualised as resulting from chronic workplace stress that has not been successfully managed. This inclusion not only validated the experiences of countless individuals suffering from burnout but also emphasised the need for systemic approaches to prevention and treatment.

Today, our understanding of burnout encompasses a wide spectrum of factors including individual personality traits, workplace culture, societal expectations, and the increasing blurring of lines between work and personal life. The condition is recognised as a global issue, affecting individuals across all professions, cultures, and levels of society. As perceptions of work and success continue to evolve in the digital age, the relevance and urgency of addressing burnout have never been clearer.

As we conclude this exploration of the historical perspectives and modern understanding of burnout, it becomes evident that this condition, far from being a mere occupational hazard, is a signal of deeper systemic issues within our work environments and societal constructs. The journey from Freudenberger's initial observations to the WHO's formal recognition underscores the complexity of burnout and the necessity of a multifaceted approach to its management.

In the next chapter, we transition from a broad overview of burnout's evolution to a focused examination of its core components. Understanding the emotional exhaustion, depersonalisation, and reduced sense of personal accomplishment that characterise burnout offers us a lens through which to view the condition not just as a symptom to be treated but as a challenge to be understood, mitigated, and, ultimately, transformed.

Multidimensional Nature of Burnout

Emotional exhaustion, the first dimension of burnout, is characterised by overwhelming fatigue and a sense of being emotionally drained by one's work. It's the feeling of having nothing left to give, often manifesting as a loss of energy, a growing sense of dread about going to work, and a pervasive lack of motivation. Individuals experiencing emotional exhaustion might find themselves disengaging from their tasks, colleagues, and even their personal interests, leading to a life that feels both stagnant and stressful. This state not only diminishes work performance but can also spill over into one's personal life, affecting relationships, hobbies, and overall life satisfaction.

Depersonalisation refers to the development of a cynical, detached attitude towards one's work and the people one serves or collaborates with. This dimension of burnout manifests as an impersonal response toward recipients of one's service, care, or instruction. In the workplace, this might appear as a lack of empathy, a dismissive attitude toward clients' or colleagues' concerns, or a sense of alienation from the work community. Depersonalisation acts as a defence mechanism against emotional exhaustion. However, it comes at a high cost, eroding the quality of service, collegial relationships, and one's sense of professionalism and ethical commitment.

Reduced personal accomplishment, the third dimension, involves a decline in one's feelings of competence and achievement in work. Individuals experiencing this aspect of burnout often report feeling ineffective, doubting the value of their work, and perceiving a lack of appreciation for their efforts. This dimension can lead to a diminished sense of personal achievement and a growing disillusionment with one's career, potentially prompting questions about one's career choices and aspirations. The erosion of confidence and satisfaction in professional capabilities can further exacerbate the other dimensions of burnout, creating a cycle that is difficult to break.

The interplay between these dimensions reveals the multifaceted nature of burnout, illustrating how it extends beyond mere job dissatisfaction or stress. Emotional exhaustion, depersonalisation, and reduced personal accomplishment together paint a picture of a condition that deeply impacts individuals' sense of self, their relationships, and their ability to find joy and fulfilment in their work and beyond.

Understanding the three dimensions of burnout as delineated by Christina Maslach provides a crucial foundation for comprehending the depth and breadth of this syndrome. These dimensions highlight the critical need for addressing each aspect to foster recovery and prevention. As we transition from examining the manifestations of burnout to exploring the "Psychological Theories Underlying Burnout," we move deeper into the root causes and contributing factors. This next chapter will delve into the psychological frameworks that explain why burnout occurs, offering insights into the interplay between individual characteristics, workplace dynamics, and broader societal pressures. By understanding these underlying theories, we can better navigate the path to mitigating burnout, moving towards intervention strategies that address its core rather than just its symptoms.

Psychological Theories Underlying Burnout

Understanding burnout requires delving into the psychological underpinnings that explain its onset, a task that brings us to the forefront of two major theories: the job demands-resources (JD-R) model and the effort-reward imbalance theory. These frameworks offer insightful perspectives on the complex interplay of workplace dynamics, personal values, and societal expectations contributing to burnout, providing a comprehensive understanding of why burnout occurs and how it can be addressed.

The JD-R model says that burnout occurs due to an imbalance between job demands and the resources available to meet those demands. Job demands refer to the physical, psychological, social, or organisational aspects of a job that require sustained effort and are therefore associated with certain physiological and psychological costs. Examples include work pressure, emotional demands, and cognitive load. Conversely, job resources are aspects of the job that help achieve work goals, reduce job demands and the associated costs, or stimulate personal growth, learning, and development. These can include autonomy, social support from colleagues and supervisors, and the availability of feedback.

When job demands exceed the resources available to manage them, the imbalance leads to stress and eventually burnout. This model highlights the critical role of workplace dynamics in burnout, underscoring the importance of a well-designed job that provides adequate resources to meet its demands.

The effort-reward imbalance theory provides another lens through which to view burnout, focusing on the relationship between the effort expended at work and the rewards received in return. Rewards can be financial, in the form of salary, socio-emotional, such as recognition and support, or career opportunities including promotion prospects and job security. According to this theory, burnout occurs when the efforts made by an individual are not adequately compensated by the rewards received.

This imbalance is particularly toxic because it violates the fundamental principle of social reciprocity, leading to feelings of injustice and disappointment. Over time, this lack of reciprocity can result in chronic stress and emotional exhaustion which are key components of burnout. The theory also emphasises the role of personal values and societal expectations, suggesting that individuals with a strong, intrinsic effort-reward expectancy are more susceptible to burnout when facing an imbalance.

Both the JD-R model and the effort-reward imbalance theory illuminate the multifaceted nature of burnout, highlighting not just the role of workplace dynamics but also the influence of personal values and societal expectations. These theories suggest that burnout can be mitigated by enhancing job resources, ensuring a fair balance between effort and reward, and aligning job demands with individual capacities and values.

Understanding these psychological theories provides a foundation for recognising the signs of burnout and implementing preventive measures. It encourages a holistic approach to workplace well-being, advocating for structural changes that address the root causes of burnout such as job redesign, creating supportive work environments, and establishing fair reward systems.

The exploration of the psychological theories underlying burnout sheds light on the complexity of its causes from the intricacies of job design and workplace culture to the deeper realms of personal values and societal norms. As we transition from understanding the roots of burnout to examining its consequences, our focus shifts to "The Impact of Burnout on Mental and Physical Health." This next chapter delves into the profound effects that burnout can have on an individual's well-being, unravelling how the chronic stress and emotional turmoil associated with burnout manifest in both mental and physical ailments. By connecting the dots between the causes and effects of burnout, we pave the way for a deeper understanding of its full spectrum of impact, highlighting the urgency of addressing this pervasive issue at both individual and systemic levels.

The Impact of Burnout on Mental and Physical Health

The journey into understanding burnout reveals both its psychological contours and profound impact on mental and physical health. By examining the impact of burnout on mental well-being—including anxiety, depression, and cognitive impairments—as well as its influence on physical health through cardiovascular risks, immune system dysfunction, and chronic fatigue, we come to an understanding of the urgency of a holistic response to this escalating issue.

Burnout exerts a significant toll on mental health, manifesting in symptoms that can profoundly disrupt an individual's quality of life.

Anxiety and depression are among the most common mental health conditions associated with burnout. Individuals experiencing burnout often report feelings of overwhelming anxiety and pervasive sadness, conditions that can severely impact personal and professional functioning. Research published in journals such as "The Lancet" and "Journal of Applied Psychology" has consistently linked burnout with elevated rates of these mental health disorders, emphasising the intertwined nature of workplace stress and psychological well-being.

Cognitive impairments also emerge as a distressing consequence of burnout, with affected individuals experiencing difficulties in concentration, memory, and decision-making. These cognitive deficits not only impair work performance but also contribute to a cycle of stress and frustration, further entrenching the burnout experience.

The impact of burnout extends beyond mental health, tremendously affecting physical well-being. A significant body of evidence links burnout to an increased risk of cardiovascular diseases including hypertension and heart disease. The stress response associated with burnout can lead to chronic inflammation and elevated blood pressure, both of which are known risk factors for cardiovascular conditions. Studies in "Psychosomatic Medicine" and other medical journals have highlighted these associations, pointing to the long-term health dangers posed by unaddressed burnout.

Furthermore, burnout can compromise the immune system, making individuals more susceptible to infections, illnesses, and prolonged recovery times. The chronic stress that characterises burnout is a known factor in immune system dysfunction, highlighting the interconnectedness of stress, burnout, and physical health.

Chronic fatigue, another hallmark of burnout, represents a pervasive sense of exhaustion that rest cannot alleviate. This fatigue transcends mere tiredness, affecting individuals' capacity to engage in daily activities and enjoy life with potential long-term implications for health and well-being.

The evidence is clear: burnout is not merely an occupational hazard but a significant health issue that demands a comprehensive response. The data underscores the necessity of recognising burnout early, implementing preventative measures, and providing support for those affected. Addressing burnout requires a multi-faceted approach that includes organisational changes, individual strategies for stress management, and societal recognition of the need for work-life balance.

Understanding the broad impact of burnout on mental and physical health sets the stage for a deeper exploration of its effects on the brain. The next chapter delves into cutting-edge research that sheds light on how chronic stress and burnout alter brain structure and function.

Neuroscientific Findings: The Brain on Burnout

As we delve deeper into the realm of burnout, the journey takes us to the very core of human biology—the brain. Recent neuroscientific studies offer a window into how burnout and chronic stress insidiously alter our brain's structure and function, revealing the profound impact these conditions have on our cognitive capabilities and emotional regulation. This chapter explores the groundbreaking research that maps the neural landscapes of burnout, providing insights into its long-term implications.

At the forefront of this exploration is the prefrontal cortex, the brain's executive centre responsible for decision-making, emotional regulation, and attention. Neuroimaging studies have shown that individuals experiencing burnout exhibit altered activity in this critical region, correlating with the cognitive impairments commonly reported such as decreased concentration, memory lapses, and reduced problem-solving capacity. The chronic stress that characterises burnout appears to overload the prefrontal cortex, diminishing its efficiency and leading to a decline in cognitive performance.

Equally impacted is the amygdala, known as the brain's alarm system, which plays a pivotal role in processing emotions and stress responses. Individuals suffering from burnout show heightened activity in the amygdala, indicating an increased emotional reactivity to stress. This heightened state not only exacerbates feelings of anxiety and irritability but can also lead to a vicious cycle of stress and burnout, further draining the brain's resources.

The connection between the prefrontal cortex and the amygdala is crucial for emotional regulation. Studies suggest that burnout might disrupt this connectivity, leading to difficulties in managing stress and controlling emotional responses. This disruption in emotional regulation mechanisms can contribute to the emotional exhaustion characteristic of burnout, making individuals feel overwhelmed and unable to cope with daily stressors.

The changes in brain structure and function associated with burnout have significant implications for how we think, feel, and behave. Cognitive functions like attention, memory, and executive function are crucial for effective performance in both personal and professional contexts. Burnout's impact on these functions can lead to decreased productivity, errors, and a sense of inadequacy, further fuelling the cycle of burnout.

On the emotional front, the heightened reactivity and diminished regulation capacity can strain personal and professional relationships, leading to social withdrawal and a sense of isolation. Understanding these neuroscientific findings is crucial for developing strategies to mitigate burnout's effects, emphasising the need for interventions that target both the cognitive and emotional dimensions of this condition.

The journey through the neuroscientific findings of burnout illuminates the tangible changes within our brains that confirm the seriousness of this condition. It's a reminder that burnout is not merely a state of mind but a physiological phenomenon that demands our attention and action.

———

Having journeyed through the intricate psychological underpinnings and the neuroscientific insights of burnout in "The Psychology of Burnout," we've laid the foundation for a deeper, more nuanced understanding of this complex condition. We've navigated the historical evolution, the pivotal theories, and the profound brain changes burnout incites, equipping ourselves with the knowledge to recognise and empathise with the struggles it entails. This exploration, rich in insight and understanding, sets the stage for our next chapter, "Signs and Symptoms of Burnout."

As we transition to this new chapter, we move from the theoretical realms into the tangible, from the general to the specific. Here, we will illuminate the myriad ways burnout manifests in individuals, translating the abstract into the concrete. This next phase of our journey is about connecting dots and identifying the outward signs that stem from the psychological and neurobiological shifts we've delved into. By learning to recognise these symptoms in ourselves or those around us, we empower ourselves with the ability to intervene early, offering support and seeking solutions. The path from understanding to recognition is a crucial one, paving the way for prevention, recovery, and ultimately, resilience. Let us continue, armed with knowledge and compassion, as we explore the signs and symptoms that signal the presence of burnout.

SIGNS AND SYMPTOMS OF BURNOUT

In the next chapter of our journey, we dive into the heart of understanding burnout's tangible manifestations. This section is an essential guide through the landscape of subtle cues and overt signals that burnout leaves in its wake. As we navigate this terrain, we aim to arm you with the knowledge to recognise these indicators—not just in the abstract, but in the context of everyday life. Through this exploration, we transform understanding into action, turning the invisible into the visible. So let's uncover the signs and symptoms that signal the presence of burnout, bridging the gap between theory and reality, and guiding you toward a path of awareness and intervention.

Physical Symptoms of Burnout

In the intricate dance between mind and body, the physical symptoms of burnout emerge as critical indicators, whispering truths about our state of well-being long before we might consciously acknowledge them. This chapter delves into the physical manifestations of burnout, often cloaked in the guise of relentless fatigue, restless nights, and fluctuating appetites. These are not merely signs of a busy life; they're the body's alarm system signalling the need for a deeper examination and care.

Chronic fatigue stands at the forefront of burnout's physical symptoms, distinguishing itself from the ordinary tiredness that a good night's sleep can cure. It is an exhaustive state where the individual feels drained of energy, rendering even the simplest tasks Herculean. This pervasive weariness serves as a stark reminder of the body's limits, urging a reevaluation of our work-life balance and the pressures we endure.

Burnout often invites sleep disturbances into our lives, from the inability to fall asleep to the frustration of frequent awakenings. The irony is palpable; when the body needs rest the most, peace eludes it.

These disturbances not only compromise our ability to recuperate but also impact our mood, judgment, and overall health, forming a vicious cycle of stress and insomnia.

Changes in appetite and weight further articulate the physical toll of burnout. For some, stress triggers overeating and weight gain while for others appetite diminishes, leading to weight loss. These changes reflect the body's attempt to cope with prolonged stress, yet they also exacerbate feelings of discomfort and dissatisfaction with oneself, adding layers to the already complex experience of burnout.

Understanding these physical symptoms is paramount. They are the body's early warning system, signalling a need for change and care. Recognising these signs allows us to take proactive steps towards addressing burnout, encouraging us to seek rest, establish healthier routines, and, most importantly, reassess the demands placed upon us.

As we navigate the physical manifestations of burnout, we begin to see how deeply intertwined our physical health is with our emotional and psychological well-being. The journey from acknowledging the body's distress signals to understanding the emotional and psychological realms of burnout is a natural progression. Just as our bodies reflect the stress and exhaustion of burnout, our minds and emotions bear their own scars. The transition to exploring the emotional and psychological symptoms of burnout invites us to look beyond the physical, delving deeper into the emotional landscape that burnout shapes within us. This exploration is not just about identifying symptoms but also understanding the holistic impact of burnout on our lives.

Emotional and Psychological Symptoms

Moving deeper into the heart of burnout, we transition to exploring the emotional and psychological terrain it shapes. This chapter unfolds the nuanced emotional and psychological indicators of burnout, revealing how it insidiously permeates our inner lives.

Burnout casts a long shadow on our emotional well-being, marked by a profound sense of helplessness. This feeling, akin to being trapped in a relentless tide, erodes the sense of agency and control, leaving individuals feeling as if they are at the mercy of their circumstances. Detachment follows - a protective yet isolating mechanism where one's connection to work, passions, and even relationships begins to wane. This emotional withdrawal serves as a buffer against the constant demands and pressures, yet in its wake, it leaves a void where engagement and fulfilment once resided.

Loss of motivation further characterises the emotional landscape of burnout. Tasks and goals that once sparked enthusiasm and drive now evoke apathy as the relentless grind dims the light of motivation. Cynicism, too, becomes a frequent companion, colouring perceptions of the job and life with a bitter hue. This cynicism isn't merely a negative attitude but a defence against repeated disappointments and unmet expectations, reflecting a deep-seated disillusionment with one's professional and personal life.

Beyond the emotional symptoms, burnout affects our psychological state, weaving a complex web of thoughts and attitudes that can profoundly impact our mental health. The psychological symptoms of burnout—such as persistent self-doubt, a feeling of inadequacy, and a diminished sense of accomplishment—mirror the emotional turmoil, creating an inner landscape marked by despair and disillusionment. These symptoms are not fleeting; they are persistent echoes of a deeper discord, signalling a crucial need for introspection, support, and change.

Understanding these emotional and psychological indicators is vital. Acknowledging them as significant red flags rather than transient moments of stress underscores the importance of addressing burnout with the seriousness it warrants. It calls for a compassionate and comprehensive approach to mental health that values well-being as much as productivity.

As we navigate the emotional and psychological symptoms of burnout, we gain insight into its profound impact on our inner world. Recognising these symptoms is a critical step in the journey toward healing and recovery. However, burnout does not only reside in our feelings and thoughts alone - it manifests in our behaviours as well. The next chapter explores how the emotional and psychological turmoil of burnout translate into observable actions and patterns.

Behavioural Changes Associated with Burnout

In the unfolding narrative of burnout, the story extends beyond one's internal tumult to manifest in tangible, behavioural shifts. This chapter delves into the observable changes that often herald the presence of burnout, painting a vivid picture of how deeply it can affect individuals.

Burnout often leads to a noticeable withdrawal from responsibilities. Tasks once approached with diligence become burdensome, leading to procrastination or neglect. This retreat from professional obligations is not a mere lapse in commitment but a sign of deeper distress, a signal that the balance between demand and capacity has been breached.

Isolation marks another significant behavioural shift as individuals grappling with burnout tend to withdraw from social interactions. This detachment from colleagues and loved ones is a double-edged sword. While it might offer a temporary reprieve from stressors, it simultaneously cuts off sources of support, deepening the sense of alienation and exacerbating the condition.

Moreover, an increased reliance on substances like alcohol, caffeine, or even non-prescribed medications can emerge as a coping mechanism. While these may offer momentary relief or a semblance of energy, they are mere palliatives, masking symptoms without addressing the root causes of burnout. Over time, this reliance can lead to additional health complications, further complicating the path to recovery.

Recognising these behavioural changes in oneself or others is a crucial first step toward addressing burnout. It requires a vigilant, compassionate look that sees beyond surface-level interpretations of laziness or disinterest, understanding instead that these behaviours signal a need for help.

Strategies for recognition include maintaining open lines of communication, creating spaces for honest dialogue about stress and well-being, and observing changes in behaviour patterns over time. It's about noticing when a colleague who once was a team player starts missing deadlines or when a loved one seems increasingly distant and disengaged from activities they once enjoyed.

Supportive interventions play a pivotal role in responding to these signs. This might involve offering to lighten the load of responsibilities, encouraging professional help, or simply being present and listening without judgment. Workplaces can implement policies that promote mental health awareness, provide access to counselling services, and foster an environment where employees feel safe to express concerns about stress and burnout.

As we navigate the behavioural manifestations of burnout, we gain a clearer understanding of its multifaceted nature. These observable changes are not standalone phenomena but are instead deeply intertwined with the cognitive symptoms that burnout engenders. The further exploration of cognitive symptoms is a natural progression in our journey. It invites us to look deeper into how burnout affects our thinking processes, decision-making abilities, and overall cognitive function. Understanding these cognitive implications offers a more comprehensive view of burnout, enabling us to address it more effectively.

Cognitive Symptoms and Decision-Making

The journey takes us through not only the emotional and behavioural corridors of burnout but also into the realm of cognitive functioning where the impact of prolonged stress and exhaustion becomes starkly evident. This chapter delves into the cognitive symptoms of burnout, shedding light on the often-overlooked aspects of mental processing that are crucial for everyday decision-making and problem-solving.

Burnout, with its insidious spread through our emotional and physical well-being, also casts a shadow over our cognitive capabilities. Difficulty concentrating, a hallmark of this condition, manifests as an inability to focus on current tasks, eventually leading to decreased productivity and a sense of frustration over uncompleted tasks. This fragmented attention not only diminishes work quality but also contributes to a growing backlog of responsibilities, perpetuating the cycle of stress and burnout.

Indecisiveness emerges from the fog of burnout as another significant obstacle. The weary mind, overwhelmed by the constant barrage of decisions required both in professional settings and daily life, finds itself paralysed, unable to choose between options. This indecision is not merely a temporary hesitation but a profound impairment that affects critical thinking and problem-solving skills, further exacerbating the sense of stagnation and defeat.

A pervasive sense of inefficacy envelops the individual, undermining self-confidence and belief in one's abilities. This cognitive symptom is particularly destructive as it strikes at the core of our identity and self-esteem, leading to questions about our competence and the value of our contributions. The erosion of self-efficacy not only hinders professional growth but also affects personal aspirations and goals.

Furthermore, the clarity of thought required for sound decision-making becomes muddled as burnout skews perceptions and priorities. The stressed mind, operating under the heavy cloud of burnout, may resort to short-term coping mechanisms at the expense of long-term well-being, choosing immediate relief over sustainable solutions. This clouded judgment can lead to poor professional decisions and strained personal relationships, further complicating an already challenging situation.

The erosion of concentration, decision-making abilities, and self-efficacy under the weight of burnout has profound consequences for our professional lives and personal relationships. Recognising these symptoms as significant indicators of burnout encourages us to seek strategies for mitigation and recovery, emphasising the importance of cognitive well-being in our overall health.

The exploration of cognitive symptoms naturally leads us to the next critical discussion: burnout's impact on work performance and relationships. This forthcoming chapter builds on our understanding of burnout's cognitive effects, examining how these symptoms manifest in decreased professional efficacy and altered dynamics in personal relationships.

Impact on Work Performance and Relationships

We've explored the physical, emotional, psychological, and behavioural manifestations of burnout, yet, the ripple effects extend far beyond these personal experiences, profoundly impacting our professional lives and personal relationships. This chapter aims to contextualise the broader implications of burnout, illustrating how it can erode the very foundations of our professional efficacy and the quality of our interpersonal connections.

Burnout acts as an insidious force within professional settings, manifesting as decreased productivity, increased errors, and a pervasive lack of satisfaction in achievements. The once vibrant drive that propelled individuals toward excellence and innovation dims, leaving in its wake a sense of stagnation and disillusionment. Tasks that once engaged and excited now seem insurmountable or devoid of meaning. This decline in productivity and quality of work not only affects the individual's career trajectory but also contributes to a broader organisational strain, affecting team dynamics and overall workplace morale.

Moreover, the cycle of burnout can lead to an increase in errors— mistakes that may not only be career-limiting but can also have significant repercussions depending on the profession. In high-stakes environments, such as healthcare or aviation, these errors can have dire consequences, further amplifying the stress and guilt experienced by the individual.

The erosion of satisfaction in one's achievements marks another critical aspect of burnout's impact on professional life. This sense of diminished accomplishment contributes to questioning one's career choices and reevaluating personal goals and aspirations, often leading to existential angst and reconsidering one's professional identity.

The repercussions of burnout extend into the fabric of our personal lives, straining relationships with partners, family members, and friends. The emotional exhaustion and irritability that accompany burnout can lead to decreased patience and empathy in interactions, fostering conflict and misunderstanding. The withdrawal and isolation, behavioural hallmarks of burnout, further exacerbate these relational strains, creating a chasm between the individual and their loved ones.

Personal relationships, often serving as a source of support and comfort, can become additional sources of stress, creating a feedback loop that deepens the impact of burnout. The individual's inability to engage fully in these relationships, to be present and connected, can lead to feelings of guilt, inadequacy, and loss, undermining the foundation of trust and mutual support that these bonds are built upon.

The interconnectedness of professional well-being and personal happiness underscores the importance of addressing burnout holistically, recognising that healing and recovery must encompass both work and home environments.

This comprehensive understanding of burnout's impact sets the stage for our next exploration of the root causes of burnout. Delving into this topic, we aim to uncover the underlying factors contributing to burnout, from organisational cultures and job demands to personal values and societal expectations. Understanding these root causes is crucial for developing effective strategies to prevent burnout, fostering environments that support well-being, and nurturing resilience in the face of stress.

ROOT CAUSES OF BURNOUT

As we peel back the layers of burnout, uncovering its myriad symptoms and manifestations, we arrive at a critical juncture in our journey: the exploration of its root causes. In the following chapters, we delve into the fertile ground from which burnout springs, examining the intricate web of organisational cultures, job demands, personal values, and societal pressures that sow the seeds of this pervasive condition.

Organisational Culture and Job Demands

In the intricate web of factors contributing to burnout, organisational culture and job demands stand out as pivotal elements, shaping the terrain of our professional lives. This chapter delves into the nuanced ways in which high-pressure environments, resource scarcity, unrealistic expectations, and a lack of support add up to create a breeding ground for burnout.

Organisational culture, the invisible yet palpable fabric that shapes the workplace experience, plays a critical role in either mitigating or exacerbating burnout. Cultures that prioritise high performance above all else, often at the expense of employee well-being, create environments where stress flourishes unchecked. When this high-pressure ethos is coupled with excessive job demands—long hours, tight deadlines, and overwhelming workloads—the risk of burnout escalates dramatically.

The scarcity of resources, whether it be staffing, time, or material support, adds another layer of challenge, forcing employees to do more with less. This constant scramble not only diminishes the quality of work but also erodes the sense of accomplishment and satisfaction, leaving individuals feeling perpetually behind and inadequate.

Unrealistic expectations, set by either management or the broader organisational culture, further contribute to this toxic mix. When success is defined by unattainable standards, employees are set up for inevitable failure, fostering feelings of disillusionment and inefficacy.

A lack of support, whether in terms of mentorship, recognition, or emotional backing, leaves employees feeling isolated in their struggles. The absence of a supportive network within the workplace can exacerbate feelings of helplessness and disconnect, key components of burnout.

Despite these challenges, some organisations have successfully navigated the path toward creating environments that are less likely to cause burnout. For instance, a tech company once plagued by high turnover rates and employee burnout initiated a comprehensive wellness program that included mandatory breaks, flexible scheduling, and access to mental health resources. Within a year, they reported a significant decrease in burnout rates and an uptick in employee satisfaction and productivity.

Another example is a famous healthcare organisation that addressed burnout by implementing team-based care models, reducing individual workload and fostering a culture of recognition and support. By redistributing tasks and ensuring that contributions were acknowledged and valued, the organisation saw a marked improvement in employee morale and reduced burnout symptoms.

These case studies illustrate the transformative power of organisational change in combating burnout. By reevaluating priorities, reallocating resources, and cultivating supportive cultures, organisations can significantly mitigate the factors that contribute to employee burnout.

The exploration of organisational culture and job demands underscores the complex interplay between workplace environments and burnout. While addressing these internal factors is crucial, the journey toward understanding burnout's roots reveals that the challenges extend beyond the office doors. The next critical discussion expands our perspective to consider how the demands of our professional lives encroach upon our personal time and space, further fuelling the burnout fire.

Work-Life Imbalance

Maintaining a harmonious work-life balance emerges as a crucial yet often elusive goal while managing personal aspirations with professional responsibilities. This chapter explores the profound impact of failing to achieve this balance, highlighting how modern work practices marked by the expectation of constant availability and the increasingly blurred lines between home and work exacerbate this challenge.

The quest for a balanced life is complicated by modern work environment demands where technological advancements have made workers accessible around the clock. This constant availability can lead to work encroaching upon personal time, diminishing the opportunity for rest, recreation, and connection with loved ones. The situation is further complicated by remote working arrangements, which while offering flexibility, often lead to longer working hours and difficulty in 'switching off' from work. The result is a pervasive sense of being stretched too thin, where neither work nor personal commitments receive the full attention they deserve, leading to a decline in overall well-being and satisfaction.

The blurring of boundaries between work and home life not only increases the risk of burnout but also impacts relationships and personal health. Without clear demarcations, individuals may find themselves working in what were once sanctuaries of relaxation and family time, eroding the quality of these vital aspects of life. The psychological toll is significant, manifesting in increased stress, anxiety, and a sense of being trapped in an endless cycle of obligations.

For individuals, strategies to promote work-life integration include setting clear boundaries around work hours, creating dedicated workspaces at home, and prioritising time for self-care and family. It's also crucial to cultivate hobbies and interests outside of work, activities that rejuvenate the spirit and provide a counterbalance to professional demands.

Organisations play a leading role in supporting work-life balance. This can be achieved through policies that respect personal time, such as limiting after-hours communication and encouraging employees to fully disengage from work during vacations. Flexible working arrangements, including compressed workweeks or the option to work remotely, can also help employees tailor their schedules to better fit personal needs. Furthermore, fostering a culture that values productivity over mere presence encourages efficiency and allows employees to focus on achieving results rather than logging extended hours.

As we navigate the complexities of work-life imbalance, it becomes clear that the path to well-being lies in the ability to integrate rather than merely balance these facets of our lives. By adopting strategies delineating work from personal time and by fostering organisational cultures that support flexibility and autonomy, individuals and companies can create environments where productivity and personal fulfilment coexist harmoniously.

Transitioning from the challenge of work-life imbalance, we move to explore another critical dimension of burnout: the lack of autonomy and control. This next section delves into how the freedom to make decisions and exert control over one's work is not merely a luxury but a necessity for psychological well-being.

Lack of Autonomy and Control

In the nuanced landscape of workplace dynamics, the concept of autonomy (having control over one's work tasks, schedules, and decisions) emerges as a critical determinant of employee well-being and satisfaction. This chapter delves into the psychological ramifications of lacking autonomy and control, a state that can precipitate feelings of helplessness and contribute significantly to burnout.

At its core, autonomy is about having the freedom to make choices and having a say in how one's work is conducted. When individuals feel they have control over their work environment and decisions, they are more likely to feel invested in the outcomes and empowered in their roles. Conversely, a lack of autonomy can lead to a sense of helplessness, a psychological state where individuals feel their actions have little effect on their environment or outcomes. This perceived lack of influence can be deeply demotivating, leading to decreased engagement, productivity, and ultimately, burnout.

The psychological impact of not having autonomy in one's work is profound. It can lead to increased stress levels as employees feel constantly subjected to the whims and dictates of others without the ability to align their work with their strengths, interests, or work-life balance needs. This misalignment can create a persistent state of tension and dissatisfaction - conditions ripe for the seeds of burnout to take root.

Empowering employees by granting them autonomy in their roles is not just a gesture of trust; it's a strategic investment in the health and productivity of the workforce. Autonomy allows individuals to harness their unique skills and insights, approach tasks creatively, and take ownership of their contributions. This sense of ownership and control can lead to increased job satisfaction as employees feel their work is meaningful and aligned with their personal and professional goals.

Moreover, autonomy supports better work-life integration, allowing employees to manage their schedules in ways that accommodate their personal lives. This flexibility is particularly crucial in today's diverse and dynamic work environments, where a one-size-fits-all approach is often more hindrance than help.

As we explore the critical role of autonomy and control in preventing burnout and enhancing job satisfaction, it becomes evident that empowering employees is a cornerstone of a healthy workplace culture. However, empowerment extends beyond merely granting autonomy; it also involves acknowledging and rewarding the contributions that employees make. The next chapter, "Insufficient Recognition and

Reward," builds on the foundation laid by autonomy, delving into how recognition and reward systems can further support employee well-being and motivation.

Insufficient Recognition and Reward

In the intricate ecosystem of the workplace, recognition and rewards serve as the lifeblood of motivation and engagement, fuelling the spirit of innovation and commitment. Yet, when these systems become misaligned, the consequences can permeate the very core of an organisation's culture, leading to burnout, demotivation, and a pervasive sense of cynicism among employees. Adequate recognition and reward systems play a crucial role in sustaining employee morale and, their absence can have detrimental effects.

Recognition validates our efforts and achievements, affirming our value within a team or organisation. When hard work and accomplishments go unnoticed, it can erode the sense of purpose and belonging, leading individuals to question the worth of their contributions. This neglect can seed doubt and demotivation, gradually disengaging employees from their roles and the organisation's mission. Moreover, the lack of a reward system that adequately compensates for effort and achievement can foster cynicism, transforming what was once passion and dedication into scepticism and detachment.

The psychological ramifications are significant. Employees who feel undervalued are more likely to experience burnout, characterised by emotional exhaustion and a diminished sense of personal accomplishment. This not only affects individual well-being but also impacts organisational health, manifesting in decreased productivity, higher turnover rates, and a deteriorating workplace atmosphere.

For organisations committed to reversing the tide of burnout and rebuilding employee engagement, reevaluating recognition and reward systems is a critical step. Effective strategies must encompass both tangible rewards, such as bonuses and promotions, and intangible forms of acknowledgement like public praise and opportunities for professional growth.

1. **Personalised Recognition**: Tailoring recognition to match individual preferences and values can amplify its impact. For some, public acknowledgement in front of peers may be most meaningful. For others, a private thank-you note or a one-on-one meeting with leadership to discuss their progress and contributions might be more appreciated.

2. **Regular Feedback Loops**: Establishing regular feedback loops ensures that recognition is timely and relevant, reinforcing positive behaviours and achievements as they occur. This ongoing dialogue between employees and management fosters a culture of appreciation and continuous improvement.

3. **Rewarding Effort and Achievement**: Developing a reward system that acknowledges both outcomes and the effort invested addresses the multifaceted nature of work. This kind of system can include performance-based bonuses, professional development opportunities, and additional time off, catering to both the professional and personal needs of employees.

4. **Creating Opportunities for Growth**: Rewards that offer opportunities for professional advancement and skill development can be particularly motivating, demonstrating an investment in the employee's future. These might include sponsorship for further education, attendance at industry conferences, or participation in leadership development programs.

As we navigate the complex terrain of recognition and reward, it becomes clear that acknowledging employee contributions is pivotal in combatting burnout and fostering a motivated workforce. However, recognition alone is not enough; it must be coupled with a sense of alignment between the job and an individual's personal values. The next chapter builds upon the understanding that for work to be truly fulfilling and for burnout to be effectively addressed, employees must find a deep sense of congruence between their professional roles and their core values.

Mismatch Between Job and Personal Values

At the heart of every individual lies a set of personal values and core beliefs that guide decisions, influence behaviours, and shape perceptions of fulfilment and success. When these intrinsic values are at odds with the nature of one's job or the ethos of the workplace, it creates a profound internal conflict. This dissonance can manifest as moral distress—a state of psychological discomfort stemming from situations where individuals feel compelled to act in ways that contradict their values. Over time, this distress can erode job satisfaction, diminish motivation, and, if left unaddressed, lead to burnout. The constant battle between adhering to one's values and meeting job demands places individuals in a perpetual state of stress, undermining their sense of integrity and purpose.

The journey through moral distress toward burnout is marked by disillusionment, frustration, and a diminishing sense of accomplishment. Individuals may find themselves questioning their career choices and even their place within the broader organisational culture. This can lead to a pervasive sense of being trapped, further exacerbating feelings of helplessness and burnout. The impact of this value mismatch extends beyond the individual, affecting team dynamics, organisational loyalty, and ultimately, the quality of work produced.

Seeking alignment between work and personal values is essential for mitigating the risk of burnout and fostering a sense of fulfilment. For individuals, this may involve:

1. **Reflective Practice**: Regularly reflecting on one's values and how they align with current work. This practice can help identify areas of mismatch and guide career decisions.

2. **Open Communication**: Engaging in open conversations with supervisors about value alignment and seeking roles or projects that resonate more closely with personal values.

3. **Professional Development**: Pursuing training or roles within the organisation that align more closely with individual values, thereby enhancing job satisfaction and engagement.

For organisations, supporting value alignment involves:

1. **Cultivating a Values-Based Culture**: Clearly articulating organisational values and ensuring they are reflected in policies, practices, and daily operations. This alignment helps attract and retain employees whose personal values resonate with the organisation's.

2. **Providing Opportunities for Value Expression**: Creating roles, projects, and teams that allow employees to work in ways that affirm their values, thereby enhancing engagement and reducing the risk of burnout.

3. **Encouraging Values Exploration**: Offering workshops and resources that help employees explore and articulate their values, fostering a deeper understanding of how their work contributes to their personal and professional growth.

The exploration of the mismatch between job and personal values concludes our journey through the root causes of burnout, underscoring the importance of alignment for both individual well-being and organisational health. As we transition from understanding the multifaceted nature of burnout to exploring strategies for recovery and prevention, the insights garnered here serve as a foundation. Recognising and addressing the misalignments between personal values and professional demands is crucial in crafting a path toward comprehensive well-being. Armed with this understanding, individuals and organisations alike can take proactive steps to foster environments where personal integrity and professional aspirations converge, paving the way for a future where burnout is not an inevitability but a challenge to overcome through awareness, alignment, and action.

PART II: THE ROAD TO RECOVERY

Part Two of this book, "The Road to Recovery," stands as a beacon of hope and renewal. Having navigated the complex terrain of the psychology behind burnout, its root causes, and its symptoms, we now embark on a transformative path toward healing, resilience, and well-being. This section is an invitation to walk through the doors of acknowledgement and acceptance to gently but firmly confront the reality of burnout and embrace the possibility of recovery.

We begin by acknowledging the power of recognition and acceptance. Understanding that acknowledging our state of burnout is not a sign of weakness but the first step towards recovery is crucial. We'll explore the transformative process of acknowledging our experiences, embracing acceptance, and preparing ourselves for the journey ahead, guided by psychological research and models of change.

The path then leads us to seek professional intervention, delving into the efficacy of various therapy approaches including Cognitive Behavioural Therapy (CBT) and Rapid Transformational Therapy (RTT). This section illuminates the role of professional support in healing from burnout, offering insights into finding the right help and embracing the process of recovery.

Finally, we'll equip ourselves with self-care strategies that foster resilience and well-being. From the grounding practice of mindfulness to the rejuvenating powers of sleep, exercise, and nutrition, this section is a treasure trove of practices that nurture our physical, emotional, and mental health.

Part Two is more than a guide; it's a companion on your journey to recovery. It's here to remind you that the road to well-being, though sometimes challenging, is paved with hope, understanding, and actionable steps toward healing. So, let's turn the page together, embarking on this transformative journey with open hearts and minds, ready to rediscover balance and joy in our lives.

ACKNOWLEDGING AND ACCEPTING

The Power of Acknowledgment

In the journey toward healing from burnout, the act of acknowledgement serves as the first, pivotal step out of the shadows of denial and isolation. This chapter delves into the profound psychological impact of acknowledging burnout, exploring how this act of courage can break the cycles that keep us bound to our exhaustion and disconnection. Through acknowledgement, we initiate a transformative process, setting the stage for recovery and renewal.

Acknowledging burnout means moving beyond mere recognition of symptoms to a deep, personal acceptance of our current state. It's about naming the experience, owning it without judgment, and understanding that it's a response to prolonged stress and not a personal failing. This step is crucial because burnout thrives in silence and isolation. The longer we deny its presence, the deeper it embeds itself into our lives, making the path to recovery increasingly obscured.

The psychological impact of this acknowledgement cannot be overstated. Breaking through denial and admitting to ourselves and others that we're struggling is liberating and empowering. It dismantles the stigma and shame often associated with burnout, opening doors to support and understanding. Psychological research underscores the healing power of acknowledgement. Studies published in the field of mental health reveal that individuals who openly acknowledge their burnout experience a significant reduction in stress and anxiety levels.

This relief often stems from the validation that comes with naming one's experience. It sends a powerful message: your feelings are real, they are valid, and you are not alone in this struggle.

Moreover, acknowledgement acts as a catalyst for action. It transitions us from a state of passivity, where burnout is something that simply happens to us, to a stance of empowerment where we can actively engage in our recovery. This shift is critical because the path to healing from burnout is not passive. It requires intentional, sustained effort and change.

As we embrace the power of acknowledgement, we prepare ourselves for the next step in our healing journey—"Understanding the Stages of Change." Acknowledging burnout is just the beginning. True recovery involves navigating through various stages of change from contemplating the need for change to preparing, acting, and maintaining new behaviours and attitudes that support our well-being. In the following section, we'll explore these stages in detail, offering insights into how each phase contributes to a comprehensive recovery process. This exploration will not only deepen our understanding of the journey ahead but also equip us with the knowledge to navigate it with purpose and resilience.

Understanding the Stages of Change

Embarking on the path to recovery from burnout is akin to navigating a journey of transformation that is deeply personal and universally understood. At the heart of this journey lies the Stages of Change model, a framework that offers a map for recognising where we stand and how we can move forward. This model, grounded in decades of psychological research, outlines a sequence of phases that individuals typically pass through on their way to making significant life changes. Understanding these stages in the context of recovering from burnout provides invaluable insights into the ebb and flow of our healing process.

Precontemplation: The journey often begins before we even recognise the need for change. In the precontemplation stage, burnout may be taking its toll, yet the acknowledgement of its impact remains out of reach. It's a stage marked by denial or unawareness, where the signs of burnout are either not recognised or minimised.

Contemplation: Recognition dawns in the contemplation stage. Here, individuals start to acknowledge the presence of burnout and consider the possibility of change. This stage is characterised by ambivalence— a tug-of-war between the desire to escape the clutches of burnout and the daunting prospect of making a change.

Preparation: Moving from contemplation to preparation signals a commitment to action. In this stage, individuals begin to gather resources, seek information, and plan their steps toward recovery. It's a time of readiness, where the decision to change starts to take shape into a tangible plan.

Action: The action stage is where change becomes visible. Steps are taken to modify behaviours, environments, or situations contributing to burnout. It might involve setting boundaries, seeking professional help, or implementing self-care routines. This stage requires considerable effort and commitment but is also where the rewards of recovery become most apparent.

Maintenance: Finally, the maintenance stage focuses on sustaining the changes made. It's about integrating new behaviours into one's life to prevent relapse. This stage is not static but an ongoing process of growth, learning, and adaptation, ensuring that the strides made towards recovery are preserved and built upon.

Navigating these stages is not a linear journey; it is a cyclical process where moving back and forth between stages is common and expected. Each stage offers unique challenges and opportunities for growth, requiring different strategies and forms of support.

As we explore the stages of change and their application to recovering from burnout, we pave the way for a deeper exploration of a critical aspect of this journey: "The Role of Acceptance in Healing." Acceptance is not about resignation but about embracing reality with openness and willingness to engage with the process of change. In the following section, we'll delve into how accepting our current state, without judgment or self-criticism, forms the bedrock of genuine healing and transformation. This acceptance is the soil from which new growth emerges, marking a pivotal point in the journey from the depths of burnout to the heights of renewed well-being.

The Role of Acceptance in Healing

Acceptance, in the context of healing from burnout, involves acknowledging our feelings, experiences, and circumstances without judgment. It's recognition of our present reality including the pain and exhaustion of burnout, coupled with an understanding that this state does not define us. Rather than pushing away our struggles or berating ourselves for not coping better, acceptance invites us to observe our situation with compassion and curiosity. This shift in perspective is crucial—it allows us to move from a stance of self-criticism to one of self-care, from a place of resistance to a position of openness to change.

The principles of Acceptance and Commitment Therapy (ACT) offer valuable insights into how acceptance can facilitate recovery from burnout. ACT posits that by embracing our thoughts and feelings rather than fighting them, we can better align our actions with our values and make meaningful changes in our lives. Research in the field of psychology supports the efficacy of ACT in addressing burnout, demonstrating that individuals who practice acceptance as part of their recovery experience significant reductions in stress, anxiety, and burnout symptoms.

By embracing our feelings and circumstances, we allow ourselves the space to understand the roots of our burnout. This understanding is essential for identifying the changes needed, whether they involve modifying our work environment, adjusting our personal habits, or seeking support. Acceptance empowers us to take these steps with a sense of purpose and self-compassion rather than out of desperation or self-reproach.

The journey of acceptance is inherently personal and can profoundly impact how we navigate the road to recovery. It teaches us that healing is not a linear process but a journey marked by moments of insight, challenge, and growth. Through acceptance, we learn to treat ourselves with the same kindness and patience we would offer a dear friend, recognising that recovery takes time and that each step forward, no matter how small, is a victory.

As we embrace acceptance in our healing journey, we also confront obstacles such as resistance and self-blame. These barriers can impede our progress, locking us in a cycle of guilt and frustration. In the next section, we'll explore strategies for overcoming resistance and self-blame, understanding that these challenges, while daunting, can be navigated with compassion and resilience. By addressing these internal hurdles, we further clear the path toward recovery, opening ourselves to the possibilities of renewal and growth.

Overcoming Resistance and Self-Blame

Resistance to change is a natural human instinct, often stemming from fear of the unknown or comfort in the familiar, even when it's detrimental to our well-being. In the context of burnout recovery, this resistance can manifest as denial of the problem or reluctance to adopt necessary changes in lifestyle or work habits. To overcome this resistance, it's essential to start small, setting achievable goals that gradually lead to more significant changes. Creating a vision of what life could look like post-recovery can also serve as a powerful motivator, helping to break through the inertia of resistance. Mindfulness practices can be particularly effective in this context, teaching us to observe our thoughts and feelings without judgment, thereby reducing the fear and anxiety that often accompany change.

Self-blame is another common barrier in the path to recovery from burnout. Many individuals internalise failure, attributing burnout solely to personal shortcomings. This self-blame not only exacerbates feelings of inadequacy but also impedes the healing process. Combatting self-blame requires a shift toward self-compassion. This involves treating oneself with the same kindness and understanding one would offer a friend in distress. Techniques such as journaling can be instrumental in this process, allowing for the expression and examination of self-critical thoughts in a safe, non-judgmental space. Additionally, engaging in positive affirmations and self-care practices can reinforce self-worth and counteract negative self-perceptions.

At the heart of overcoming resistance and self-blame lies the practice of self-compassion and forgiveness. Self-compassion involves acknowledging our suffering, recognising its common humanity, and being kind to ourselves. Forgiveness, specifically self-forgiveness, allows us to release the burden of past mistakes and move forward with greater ease. Research has shown that individuals who cultivate self-compassion and forgiveness experience lower levels of psychological distress and are better equipped to navigate the challenges of recovery from burnout.

Cultivating self-compassion and practising forgiveness are not just strategies for overcoming barriers. They are foundational principles of the acceptance process. They remind us that healing from burnout is as much about repairing our relationship with ourselves as it is about changing our external circumstances.

As we navigate through resistance, self-blame, and the journey toward self-compassion, we also recognise the importance of the environment in which this process unfolds. Creating a supportive environment for acknowledgement—a space where our experiences and feelings are validated by those around us—can significantly enhance our ability to embrace acceptance and move forward. In the next section, we'll explore how to cultivate such an environment, drawing on the strength of our communities, relationships, and professional networks to bolster our journey of recovery.

Creating a Supportive Environment for Acknowledgment

Beyond the internal work of acknowledgement and acceptance lies the crucial need for a supportive network—a sanctuary of friends, family, and professionals who offer validation, encouragement, and understanding.

The significance of cultivating a supportive network cannot be overstated. Human beings are inherently social creatures, and our interactions with those around us have a profound impact on our psychological health.

In the context of burnout recovery, a supportive network acts as a buffer against the isolation and despair that often accompany this condition. Friends and family can provide a listening ear, a shoulder to lean on, and a dose of perspective when we're too close to our struggles to see clearly. Similarly, professionals—be they therapists, counsellors, or coaches—bring expertise and objectivity, guiding us through the recovery process with tailored advice and strategies.

Opening up about our experiences with burnout requires courage and vulnerability. To foster an environment of understanding and support, clear communication is key. It involves expressing our feelings and needs honestly while setting boundaries to protect our well-being. Here are some strategies to enhance communication:

1. **Use "I" Statements**: Frame your experiences and needs from your perspective to avoid blame and facilitate understanding.

2. **Be Specific**: Clearly articulate what support you need, whether it's someone to listen, help with specific tasks, or professional guidance.

3. **Seek Mutual Understanding**: Encourage open dialogue, allowing others to share their thoughts and feelings, fostering a two-way street of support and empathy.

Creating such an environment not only aids in the healing process but also strengthens our relationships, building a foundation of trust and mutual support that can withstand the challenges of burnout recovery.

Encouraging friends, family, and professionals to learn about burnout can enhance their ability to provide meaningful support. Sharing resources and articles or even inviting them to therapy sessions (with consent) can illuminate the complexities of burnout, enabling them to offer more targeted and empathetic support.

As we conclude this exploration of acknowledging and accepting burnout, we stand at the cusp of transformation. This initial phase of recovery, marked by the courage to face our burnout and the wisdom to seek support, lays the groundwork for the journey ahead. It teaches us that healing is not a solitary endeavour but a communal voyage, enriched by the empathy, understanding, and encouragement of those around us. As we move forward, let us carry the lessons of acknowledgement and acceptance with us, allowing them to light our path toward recovery.

Transitioning from the foundational steps of acknowledging and accepting, we venture into the realm of "Professional Intervention."

This next phase of our journey delves into the therapeutic landscapes that offer guidance and strategies for healing. From Cognitive Behavioural Therapy (CBT) to Rapid Transformational Therapy (RTT), we'll explore the diverse avenues of professional support, each offering a beacon of hope. As we embark on this exploration, remember that seeking professional help is not just an important step but a leap toward reclaiming our vitality and joy.

PROFESSIONAL INTERVENTION

As we journey deeper into the heart of recovery, this chapter opens the door to exploring the pivotal role that expert guidance plays in our path to healing from burnout. This section illuminates the myriad of therapeutic approaches and professional support available from the transformative powers of Cognitive Behavioural Therapy (CBT) and Rapid Transformational Therapy (RTT) to the personalised touch of counselling and coaching. Here, we demystify the process of seeking help, offering insights and encouragement to embrace professional intervention not as a last resort but as a courageous step towards reclaiming your well-being and vitality. Together, we'll navigate the landscape of professional support, discovering how it can be a cornerstone in building a more resilient, joyful self.

Understanding the Role of Professional Support

There comes a pivotal moment in the recovery from burnout when self-management strategies alone may not suffice. It's at this juncture that the concept of professional intervention becomes not just relevant, but crucial. Embracing professional support is a courageous step, an acknowledgement that your journey to well-being might require expertise beyond your own.

Professional intervention encompasses a broad spectrum of services, from psychological counselling and therapy to coaching and psychiatric help, tailored to address the multifaceted nature of burnout. The essence of seeking professional help lies in the recognition that burnout, with its complex web of psychological, physical, and emotional strands, often necessitates a nuanced approach to healing. It's about understanding that the journey back to wellness sometimes requires a map that only a trained guide can provide.

One of the paramount benefits of professional intervention is the development of personalised care plans. These plans are not one-size-fits-all but are meticulously crafted to meet your unique needs, challenges, and goals. They consider the specific nuances of your burnout experience, ensuring that the path to recovery is as individualised as the factors that led to your burnout.

Expert advice, grounded in years of research and clinical experience, offers insights and strategies that might not be accessible through general self-help resources. Professionals bring a wealth of knowledge about the latest treatments, therapeutic techniques, and holistic approaches to recovery. This expertise becomes invaluable in navigating the complexities of burnout, providing clarity and direction where before there might have been confusion and uncertainty.

One of the most profound benefits is the relief that comes from sharing the burden. Burnout can feel like a solitary struggle, a weight that you carry alone. Engaging with a professional creates a shared space of understanding and empathy, where your experiences are validated, and your feelings are acknowledged. This act of sharing can lighten the emotional load, making the path to recovery feel less daunting and more manageable.

The decision to seek professional help is a significant, sometimes challenging step on the road to recovery. It requires vulnerability and trust—vulnerability in exposing your struggles, and trust in the professional guiding you through them. Yet, it is within this space of openness and expert support that many find the keys to unlocking a more balanced, healthy state of being.

As we contemplate the pivotal role of professional support in navigating burnout, our exploration naturally leads us to specific therapeutic approaches that have shown promise in the recovery process. In the next part of this book, we will dive into the world of Cognitive Behavioural Therapy (CBT) and Rapid Transformational Therapy (RTT). We'll uncover how these methodologies offer unique perspectives and tools for managing the symptoms of burnout, inviting us to view our recovery through a lens of empowerment and hope.

Exploring Therapy Approaches: CBT and RTT

In the landscape of recovery from burnout, the terrain is diverse and the paths to healing are many. Among the most effective and transformative therapeutic approaches stand Cognitive Behavioural Therapy (CBT) and Rapid Transformational Therapy (RTT). Each offers unique insights and strategies for overcoming burnout, tailored to meet individuals at their point of need and guide them toward renewal.

Cognitive Behavioural Therapy, a well-established form of psychotherapy, operates on the fundamental belief that our thoughts, feelings, and behaviours are interconnected. The crux of CBT lies in its focus on identifying and challenging negative thought patterns and beliefs that contribute to burnout, thereby altering maladaptive behaviours and emotions. It equips individuals with practical skills to manage stress more effectively, fostering a healthier perspective on work and life challenges.

CBT's efficacy in treating burnout is well-documented. Recent studies have shown that individuals who undergo CBT report significant reductions in symptoms of burnout, including emotional exhaustion, increased mental distance from their job, and a decline in productivity. By addressing the cognitive distortions that often accompany burnout such as perfectionism, catastrophic thinking, and black-and-white thinking, CBT helps individuals cultivate a more balanced and realistic outlook.

The structured nature of CBT, typically involving goal-oriented sessions, makes it an empowering process. Individuals learn to identify their stress triggers, develop coping strategies, and reframe their thoughts in a way that promotes resilience and well-being. This active, hands-on approach to recovery is particularly effective for those seeking to regain control over their burnout experience and chart a course toward lasting change.

Rapid Transformational Therapy, a newer yet increasingly popular therapeutic approach, offers a different path to healing. RTT combines the principles of hypnotherapy with unique techniques to access the subconscious mind, aiming to uncover and address the root causes of burnout. This approach is grounded in the understanding that our subconscious beliefs significantly influence our thoughts, feelings, and behaviours, often in ways we're not consciously aware of.

Through RTT, individuals are guided into a state of deep relaxation where they can explore and understand the subconscious drivers behind their burnout. This might include unresolved issues, limiting beliefs, or past experiences that have contributed to their current state. By bringing these to light, RTT facilitates a rapid rewiring of the subconscious mind, allowing individuals to release these blockages and adopt more empowering beliefs and behaviours.

The success stories of RTT are compelling with many individuals reporting breakthroughs in just a few sessions. Clients often describe a newfound sense of freedom and empowerment as they're able to let go of the subconscious narratives that have held them back. This swift transformation is particularly appealing for those who feel stuck in their burnout cycle, offering a beacon of hope for rapid and profound change.

As we delve into the intricacies of CBT and RTT, it becomes clear that the journey of recovery from burnout is deeply personal with each individual requiring a tailored approach to healing. While these therapies offer powerful frameworks for change, the role of personalised support cannot be understated. This leads us to the next critical piece of the recovery puzzle: the value of counselling and coaching. We will explore how these personalised forms of support can complement and enhance the therapeutic process, offering individuals the guidance, accountability, and encouragement needed to navigate their way back to well-being. Whether through the structured approach of counselling or the goal-oriented focus of coaching, this next section will highlight the importance of finding the right support system to champion one's recovery from burnout.

The Value of Counselling and Coaching

As we journey deeper into the heart of recovery, the significance of personalised support becomes ever more apparent. Counselling and coaching emerge as two distinct yet complementary ways for guidance, each offering unique benefits to those navigating the path back from burnout.

Counselling provides a safe and confidential space for individuals to explore the deeper emotional undercurrents of burnout. It's an opportunity to delve into personal history, beliefs, and feelings that contribute to the experience of burnout. Counselors offer empathy, understanding, and psychological expertise, guiding clients through the complexities of their emotions and helping them uncover insights that lead to healing. The therapeutic relationship is central to counselling, offering a foundation of trust and acceptance that fosters profound emotional growth and understanding.

For those engulfed in the shadows of burnout, counselling can illuminate the path to self-awareness and emotional liberation. Through sessions that may explore past traumas, unresolved conflicts, or detrimental self-beliefs, individuals are empowered to confront and reframe the narratives that have led to their current state. The process is often transformative in alleviating burnout symptoms while also fostering a deeper connection with oneself.

In contrast, **coaching** takes a more goal-oriented approach, focusing on the present and the future rather than delving into the past. Coaches work with clients to identify specific outcomes they wish to achieve and develop actionable strategies to reach these goals. The emphasis is on practical solutions, accountability, and positive action. Coaching is particularly effective for individuals who have a clear vision of what they want to overcome or achieve but need structure and motivation to make it happen.

Coaching sessions often revolve around setting realistic, achievable goals, breaking them down into actionable steps, and identifying potential obstacles. Coaches provide the tools and support to navigate these challenges, fostering resilience and adaptability. For someone recovering from burnout, coaching can reignite a sense of purpose and direction, setting the stage for a future where well-being and professional fulfilment coexist.

The stories of those who have journeyed through counselling and coaching speak volumes about their transformative power.

Maria (47), a healthcare professional, found herself overwhelmed by burnout, struggling with emotional exhaustion and a sense of detachment from her work. Through counselling, she was able to address the guilt and perfectionism that fuelled her burnout. The process helped her develop healthier coping mechanisms and rebuild her connection to her profession, leading to a renewed sense of purpose and well-being.

Alex (37), an entrepreneur facing burnout due to the pressures of running a startup, turned to coaching for support. The process enabled him to set clear, achievable goals for managing his workload, prioritise self-care, and delegate responsibilities more effectively. Coaching transformed Alex's approach to work and life, helping him find balance and reigniting his passion for his business.

As we explore the transformative potential of counselling and coaching, it becomes evident that selecting the right professional is crucial to the success of these interventions. The journey of recovery from burnout is deeply personal, and the therapeutic alliance—be it with a counsellor or coach—plays a pivotal role in facilitating healing.

Navigating the Selection of a Professional

Selecting the right professional for guidance through the journey of recovery from burnout is akin to choosing a companion for a deeply personal voyage. The significance of this choice cannot be overstated, as the therapeutic alliance formed between you and your chosen professional is foundational to the healing process. This chapter offers practical advice on navigating the selection of a therapist, counsellor, or coach, ensuring that the partnership is not only effective but transformative.

Credentials and Specialisations: Begin by considering the credentials and specialisations of potential professionals. Look for qualifications that align with your needs—therapists and counsellors should have recognised certifications and licenses in mental health fields. For coaches, seek out those with reputable training and credentials in coaching practices. Specialisations in burnout, stress management, or your specific industry can provide added insight and relevance to your recovery journey.

Questions to Ask: Initial consultations or discovery sessions are your opportunity to ask questions. Inquire about their experience with burnout, their approach to therapy or coaching, and success stories. Ask about their availability, session formats, and communication style. Questions like, "How do you tailor your approach to individual needs?" or "Can you describe a success story that resonates with my situation?" can provide valuable insights.

Gauging a Good Fit: A good fit goes beyond credentials and experience; it's about personal comfort and connection. Reflect on how you feel during your interactions—do you feel heard and understood? Is there a sense of trust and rapport? Your intuition about feeling safe and comfortable with a professional is a crucial indicator of a good fit. Trust in this therapeutic relationship is essential for open, honest communication and the work ahead.

The therapeutic alliance is a cornerstone of successful intervention. Research in psychotherapy outcomes consistently highlights the therapeutic alliance as a critical determinant of therapy's effectiveness. This relationship provides the secure foundation necessary for exploring vulnerabilities, challenging existing patterns, and implementing changes. A strong alliance ensures you feel supported and empowered throughout the recovery process, making the journey less daunting and more achievable.

While finding the right professional is a critical step on the road to recovery, it is equally important to recognise that this is a partnership. The next section explores how to blend the guidance received from professionals with your own initiatives and self-care practices. This integration is key to creating a comprehensive and sustainable recovery plan that empowers you to reclaim your well-being and prevent future burnout. Together, professional support and personal efforts form the dual engines that propel you forward on your journey to recovery, each enhancing and amplifying the other's impact.

Integrating Professional Help with Personal Efforts

The integration of professional guidance with self-care practices is akin to weaving a tapestry of wellness where each thread strengthens and supports the other. To achieve this harmonious blend, consider the following strategies:

Complementary Practices: Align self-care activities with the therapeutic goals set by your professional. If stress management is a focus, incorporate relaxation techniques like mindfulness or yoga into your routine. This alignment ensures that your personal efforts reinforce the therapeutic work, creating a cohesive strategy for recovery.

Personalised Self-Care Plan: Work with your therapist or coach to develop a self-care plan that resonates with your unique needs, interests, and lifestyle. This personalised plan should address physical, emotional, and mental health aspects, ensuring a comprehensive approach to well-being.

Incorporate Insights into Daily Life: Apply insights and coping strategies learned during sessions into your daily routine. This practical application of therapy or coaching can help solidify new patterns of thinking and behaviour, enhancing the overall recovery process.

Being an active participant in one's recovery journey is pivotal. It involves taking ownership of the healing process and engaging fully with both professional intervention and self-care practices.

Setting Realistic Goals: Work with your professional to set achievable, measurable goals. These goals should challenge you but also be attainable, fostering a sense of progress and accomplishment that motivates further effort.

Open Communication: Maintain transparent communication with your therapist or coach. Share your experiences, successes, and challenges openly, allowing for adjustments to your care plan that better suit your evolving needs. This collaborative approach ensures that your professional support remains relevant and responsive to your journey.

Self-Monitoring and Reflection: Regularly reflect on your progress, acknowledging growth and identifying areas for further development. This self-monitoring enhances your self-awareness and allows you to take proactive steps in your recovery.

We've explored the transformative potential of seeking professional support in the battle against burnout. From understanding the role of professional help to navigating the selection of a therapist or coach and effectively integrating this support with personal self-care efforts, this part of the book underscores the importance of a comprehensive and collaborative approach to recovery. The journey from burnout to renewal is deeply personal, yet, it is professional guidance combined with individual dedication and self-care that paves the way for a successful and sustainable healing process.

As we close this chapter on professional intervention, we prepare to embark on the next crucial phase of our journey - "Self-Care Strategies." This upcoming section will shift our focus toward the practical, everyday actions and decisions that fortify our mental, emotional, and physical health. We'll delve into self-care practices that not only complement the work done in therapy or coaching but also empower us to maintain and enhance our well-being independently. Embracing self-care is about taking control of our healing journey, one day and one choice at a time, as we continue to build a life of balance, fulfilment, and resilience.

SELF-CARE STRATEGIES

Now, let's shift our focus towards the empowering realm of self-care and highlight practices that support the healing process from burnout while also fostering long-term well-being. Self-care is an essential complement to professional intervention, offering tools and habits that individuals can adopt to nurture their mental, emotional, and physical health.

Mindfulness and Meditation

In the heart of our journey through recovery from burnout, we discover a beacon of light in the practices of mindfulness and meditation. These ancient techniques, refined through centuries, stand today as powerful tools in our modern battle against stress and burnout. They invite us into a world of increased self-awareness and inner peace, offering a sanctuary where we can learn to manage stress with grace and enhance our understanding of ourselves.

Mindfulness, the art of being fully present in the moment, teaches us to observe our thoughts, feelings, and sensations without judgment. **Meditation**, a practice that often accompanies mindfulness, provides a structured approach to quieting the mind and fostering calmness. Together, they offer a dual pathway to managing stress and cultivating an environment within ourselves that is conducive to healing and growth.

Integrating mindfulness and meditation into daily routines doesn't require hours of silent contemplation. Instead, it's about finding moments of mindfulness in everyday activities—taking a deep, conscious breath before starting your car, feeling the water on your skin during a shower, or simply being fully present with a loved one. These practices anchor us in the now, reducing the stress that comes from ruminating on the past or worrying about the future.

For those new to these practices or looking to deepen their journey, here are a few simple exercises to get started.

Mindful Breathing: Focus on your breath, observing its natural flow in and out of your body. When your mind wanders, gently guide it back to your breath. This practice can be a calming anchor, bringing you back to the present moment.

Body Scan Meditation: Lie down comfortably and slowly bring your attention to different parts of your body from your toes to your head. Notice any sensations, tension, or relaxation without trying to change anything. This technique fosters bodily awareness and releases physical stress.

Mindful Walking: Take a walk and focus on the experience of walking. Feel the ground beneath your feet, the air on your skin, and any sounds around you. This practice can transform a simple walk into a profound exercise in mindfulness.

Gratitude Meditation: Reflect on things you're grateful for. This can shift your mindset from one of lack to one of abundance, reducing stress and fostering a sense of well-being.

Research has illuminated the significant benefits of mindfulness and meditation in the context of burnout recovery. Studies published in peer-reviewed journals such as "Mindfulness" have shown that regular mindfulness practice can lead to decreased stress levels, improved emotional regulation, and enhanced overall well-being. Participants in these studies reported feeling more grounded, less overwhelmed by the pressures of work and life, and more capable of handling stress constructively.

Moreover, mindfulness has been linked to structural changes in the brain associated with attention, emotion regulation, and self-awareness. These changes not only contribute to a reduction in burnout symptoms but also enhance cognitive functions, making mindfulness a potent tool for both recovery and personal development.

As we embrace the practices of mindfulness and meditation, we fortify our mental and emotional defences against burnout. However, the journey to recovery encompasses more than just our inner landscape; it also involves nurturing our physical body. The next chapter, "Physical Exercise for Mental Health," will explore how engaging in physical activity can complement our mindfulness practices, further reducing stress and enhancing our resilience. Exercise, like mindfulness, is a powerful ally in our recovery from burnout, offering a holistic approach to restoring our well-being and vitality. Together, mindfulness and physical exercise form a synergistic duo, each amplifying the benefits of the other and paving the way for a balanced, healthy life.

Physical Exercise for Mental Health

Within the tapestry of strategies for recovering from burnout, physical exercise emerges as a vibrant thread, weaving together the physical and mental aspects of our well-being. The benefits of regular physical activity extend far beyond the confines of physical health, playing a pivotal role in alleviating mental stress and enhancing our mood and cognitive function.

Physical exercise is a natural antidote to stress, capable of dissolving tension as if it were smoke carried away by the wind. It stimulates the production of endorphins, often referred to as the body's feel-good hormones, which act as natural painkillers and mood elevators. Regular engagement in physical activity has been shown to improve mood, enhance cognitive function, and reduce symptoms of anxiety and depression, creating a stronger, more resilient foundation against the pressures that contribute to burnout.

Moreover, exercise plays a significant role in improving sleep quality and concentration, further enhancing its status as a cornerstone of mental health. By alleviating physical tension, exercise facilitates relaxation and mental clarity, offering a much-needed reprieve from the incessant demands of daily life.

Incorporating exercise into daily life is a journey that begins with a single step, literally and metaphorically. It's about finding activities that resonate with your interests and fit into your lifestyle, creating a sustainable routine that brings joy and vitality. Here are some suggestions for integrating exercise into your life, tailored to accommodate various fitness levels:

Start with Walking: A simple walk, whether in a park, around the neighbourhood, or even during lunch breaks, can be a powerful entry point into the world of physical activity. It's low impact, accessible, and can be a meditative practice in mindfulness.

Explore Yoga: Yoga offers a combination of physical postures, breathing exercises, and meditation, making it an excellent choice for those seeking a holistic approach to exercise. It's adaptable to all fitness levels and can be practised at home or in a class setting.

Try Home Workouts: With a plethora of online resources available from fitness apps to YouTube channels, home workouts can be customised to fit any schedule, preference, and fitness level. They provide a convenient way to stay active without the need for gym access.

Engage in Vigorous Sports: For those seeking more intense physical activity, sports like cycling, running, swimming, or team sports offer not just physical exertion but the added benefit of community and fun.

Various researches underscore the effectiveness of exercise in mitigating burnout and enhancing well-being. Studies published in reputable journals such as "The American Journal of Preventive Medicine" have demonstrated that regular physical activity is associated with lower levels of job burnout and perceived stress. Furthermore, individuals who maintain an active lifestyle report higher levels of job satisfaction and overall happiness, illustrating exercise's comprehensive benefits on mental and emotional health.

These studies highlight not just the physical benefits of exercise, but its profound impact on our psychological state, offering a compelling argument for its inclusion in any burnout recovery plan.

As we recognise the transformative power of physical exercise in our recovery from burnout, it's essential to remember that our bodies' needs extend beyond movement. The next chapter will explore how the foods we consume play an equally crucial role in our mental and physical health. Just as exercise strengthens and revitalises our bodies, a balanced diet nourishes our system, providing the essential nutrients needed to support our recovery journey. Together, exercise and nutrition form a synergistic duo, each enhancing the effectiveness of the other and paving the way for a holistic approach to overcoming burnout.

Nutritional Well-being

Navigating the path to recovery from burnout involves more than just addressing our mental and emotional needs; it requires us to look closely at the fuel we provide our bodies. The profound impact of diet on mental health is a topic garnering increasing attention as research continues to reveal the intricate connections between what we eat, how we feel, and how we think.

Our brains, those complex command centres, require a variety of nutrients to function optimally. The relationship between diet and mental health is bidirectional; just as stress and emotional turmoil can lead to changes in eating habits, what we consume can significantly influence our mood, stress levels, and overall mental well-being. Foods rich in vitamins, minerals, and antioxidants can protect the brain from oxidative stress, while a diet lacking essential nutrients can exacerbate symptoms of burnout, leading to increased anxiety and fatigue.

For those on the path to recovery from burnout, embracing a diet that supports mental well-being is essential. Here are some guidelines to help you nourish your body and mind:

Foods to Embrace:

Omega-3 Rich Foods: Incorporate sources of omega-3 fatty acids, such as salmon, walnuts, and flaxseeds, which are known to reduce inflammation and support cognitive function and mood regulation.

Antioxidant-Rich Fruits and Vegetables: Consume a colourful array of fruits and vegetables, packed with antioxidants that protect brain cells from damage and support overall health.

Whole Grains: Opt for whole grains like oats, quinoa, and brown rice, which provide steady energy and help regulate blood sugar levels, reducing mood swings and fatigue.

Lean Proteins: Include lean protein sources, such as chicken, turkey, beans, and lentils, which contain amino acids essential for neurotransmitter function and energy levels.

Foods to Avoid:

High Sugar and Processed Foods: Limit intake of sugary snacks, beverages, and processed foods, which can lead to energy crashes and exacerbate symptoms of anxiety and depression.

Caffeine and Alcohol: While it may be tempting to rely on caffeine for an energy boost or alcohol to unwind, both can interfere with sleep patterns and mood stability and should be consumed in moderation.

The research underscores the link between diet and mental health, with numerous studies highlighting how nutritional interventions can reduce symptoms of burnout and improve well-being. For instance, studies published in "Nutritional Neuroscience" have shown that diets high in fruits, vegetables, and omega-3 fatty acids can lead to improvements in mood and reductions in stress levels among participants. Additionally, dietary patterns that emphasise whole foods over processed options have been associated with lower rates of depression and anxiety, further supporting the role of nutrition in mental health recovery.

As we consider the vital role of nutrition in our recovery from burnout, it's important to recognise that what we eat is just one piece of the puzzle. Another foundational aspect of our well-being, deeply intertwined with our dietary habits, is the quality of our sleep. Restorative sleep is crucial for mental and physical health. Together, nutritional well-being and quality sleep form a synergistic duo, each enhancing the benefits of the other and laying the groundwork for a holistic approach to recovery from burnout.

Quality Sleep as a Foundation

Sleep and burnout share a reciprocal relationship; just as burnout can lead to sleep disturbances, inadequate sleep can intensify the symptoms of burnout, creating a vicious cycle. Sleep deprivation impacts cognitive function, emotional regulation, and physical health, magnifying feelings of exhaustion, cynicism, and inefficacy. Conversely, quality sleep acts as a healing balm, supporting the body's repair processes, consolidating memories, and regulating emotions, thereby fortifying our resilience against stress.

Improving sleep hygiene involves adopting practices that promote consistent, restful sleep. Here are some strategies to cultivate better sleep habits:

- **Establish a Regular Sleep Schedule:** Aim for a consistent bedtime and wake-up time, even on weekends, to regulate your body's internal clock.

- **Create a Restful Environment:** Ensure your bedroom is conducive to sleep—quiet, dark, and cool. Consider the use of white noise machines or blackout curtains to enhance your sleep environment.

- **Limit Exposure to Screens:** Reduce blue light exposure from phones, tablets, and computers at least an hour before bedtime, as it can interfere with melatonin production and disrupt sleep.

- **Mindful Evening Routines:** Engage in relaxing activities before bed, such as reading, gentle yoga, or a warm bath, to signal your body that it's time to wind down.

- **Manage Caffeine and Alcohol Intake:** Limit caffeine consumption in the afternoon and evening and moderate alcohol intake, as both can affect sleep quality.

Recent studies underscore the critical role of sleep in the context of burnout recovery. For instance, research published in the "Journal of Applied Psychology" found that individuals reporting higher sleep quality showed significant improvements in burnout symptoms over time, compared to those with poor sleep patterns. Another study in "Sleep Medicine Reviews" highlighted that interventions aimed at improving sleep can lead to reductions in workplace stress and burnout levels, demonstrating the efficacy of sleep-focused strategies in enhancing overall well-being.

These findings reinforce the notion that investing in sleep is investing in our capacity to thrive, underscoring the importance of prioritising rest as part of a comprehensive approach to recovering from burnout.

In summarising the journey through the landscape of sleep's role in burnout recovery, it's clear that quality rest is not just a luxury but a necessity. By embracing strategies that promote restorative sleep, we lay the groundwork for a resilient, balanced life -one where burnout's shadows recede in the light of our renewed energy and vitality.

Throughout the chapters dedicated to self-care, we've traversed a path lined with powerful tools for self-renewal and healing. From the mindful tranquillity of meditation and the vibrant energy of physical exercise to the nourishing power of a balanced diet and the restorative embrace of quality sleep, each strategy has been a beacon of hope on the road to recovery from burnout. These practices not only offer relief from the immediate symptoms of burnout but also fortify our defences against future stressors. As we close this chapter, let us carry forward the understanding that self-care is the most profound act of self-respect—a commitment to nurturing the well-being that empowers us to live fully, passionately, and resiliently in the face of life's inevitable challenges.

Conclusion

Part Two of our journey, "The Road to Recovery," has been a deep dive into the heart of healing from burnout, exploring the multifaceted approaches that pave the way toward renewal and resilience. This comprehensive exploration has provided us with a roadmap, marked by signs of understanding, intervention, and self-care, guiding us through the varied landscapes of recovery. Let's take a moment to reflect on the ground we've covered, distilling the essence of our journey and preparing ourselves for the next section: "Prevention and Sustainable Well-Being."

Our journey began with the foundational steps of acknowledging and accepting burnout. We discovered the transformative power of recognising our state not as a sign of weakness, but as a courageous step toward healing. Through the lens of acceptance, we learned to view our experience with compassion and understanding, breaking the chains of denial and self-blame. This phase reminded us that healing starts with an honest conversation with ourselves, acknowledging our limits, and embracing our need for change.

Navigating the terrain of burnout, we recognised when to seek the guidance of professionals. Exploring the realms of Cognitive Behavioural Therapy (CBT) and Rapid Transformational Therapy (RTT), we understood how specialised interventions can offer new perspectives and strategies for dealing with stress and exhaustion. Counselling and coaching emerged as vital allies, providing us with the support and accountability needed to implement meaningful changes. This segment underscored the importance of finding the right professional—a partnership built on trust and understanding, critical for our journey toward recovery.

Perhaps the most empowering aspect of our journey has been the exploration of self-care strategies. We delved into mindfulness and meditation, uncovering their capacity to ground us in the present and alleviate the weight of our worries. Physical exercise was highlighted as a powerful antidote to stress, able to improve both our mental and physical health. Nutritional well-being taught us how the right foods could be our allies in combating burnout, and nourishing our bodies and minds. And in the sanctuary of sleep, we found the ultimate restoration, learning strategies to improve the quality of our rest and, by extension, our resilience against burnout.

Together, these strategies weave a tapestry of recovery, each thread reinforcing the others, creating a stronger, more vibrant, picture of well-being. This journey has not been about quick fixes but building a sustainable practice of self-awareness, professional support, and self-care. We've learned that recovery from burnout is as much about healing our present wounds as it is about nurturing our future selves, laying the groundwork for a life that not only survives but thrives.

As we stand on the precipice of Part Three, "Prevention and Sustainable Well-Being," we carry with us the lessons learned on the road to recovery. The journey ahead is one of proactive engagement with our lives, crafting an existence that prioritises balance, fulfilment, and resilience. We move forward with a renewed sense of purpose, understanding that preventing burnout is not merely about avoiding stress but about creating a life that aligns with our deepest values and aspirations.

In this next chapter, we will explore strategies for embedding prevention into the fabric of our daily lives from cultivating habits that support physical and mental health to fostering environments that encourage well-being. We'll learn how to set boundaries that protect our energy, engage in work that nurtures our souls, and build communities that uplift and support us. The path to sustainable well-being is a personal and collective journey, one that invites us to reimagine our lives in ways that bring joy, purpose, and peace.

As we transition to this new phase, let us embrace the opportunity to not just recover from burnout but to reinvent our approach to living. Together, we'll discover how to sustain the well-being we've worked so hard to achieve, ensuring that the life we build is resilient, joyful, and deeply fulfilling.

PART III: PREVENTION AND SUSTAINABLE WELL-BEING

As we step into Part Three of our transformative journey, "Prevention and Sustainable Well-Being," we embark on perhaps the most empowering phase of our quest to recover from burnout and thrive beyond it. Having navigated the depths of acknowledging our burnout and exploring the avenues of professional intervention and self-care strategies, we now stand at the threshold of a new chapter—one that focuses on proactively crafting a life that sustains and nurtures our well-being in every facet.

This section of the book is dedicated to the art of prevention, a proactive approach to well-being that goes beyond mere recovery. It's about building a foundation so strong that the tremors of stress and exhaustion find it difficult to shake. Prevention is not just about avoiding burnout; it's about creating a life filled with joy, purpose, and balance.

In these pages, we'll explore the pillars of sustainable well-being from cultivating habits that support our physical and mental health to creating environments that inspire and uplift us. We'll delve into the importance of setting boundaries that protect our energy, engaging in work that fulfils us, and fostering relationships that provide support and connection. Each strategy and insight is designed to guide you in building a resilient, joyous life where well-being is not an afterthought but a priority.

This journey is both personal and universal. It's about discovering what uniquely sustains you while also recognising the common threads that bind us all in our search for a meaningful, balanced life. Whether you're looking to reinforce your recovery from burnout or proactively safeguard your well-being, this section offers a roadmap for embedding wellness into the essence of who you are and how you live.

PERSONAL HABITS FOR LONG-TERM BALANCE

In the final leg of our journey toward a burnout-resistant lifestyle, we lay the groundwork for establishing personal habits that contribute to a life of balance, joy, and resilience. By focusing on mindfulness, routine, physical activity, nutrition, and rest, we equip ourselves with the tools needed to build a foundation of sustainable well-being.

Mindfulness as a Daily Practice

In our pursuit of a life resilient against burnout, embracing mindfulness as a daily practice emerges as a cornerstone of sustainable well-being. This chapter delves into the transformative benefits of mindfulness, a simple yet profound approach to living that encourages us to engage fully with the present moment. By utilising mindfulness in our daily routines, we unlock a powerful tool for enhancing awareness, reducing stress, and fostering a deep sense of peace and clarity amidst life's inevitable turbulence.

Mindfulness, the art of maintaining a moment-by-moment awareness of our thoughts, feelings, bodily sensations, and the surrounding environment, offers a pathway to reducing the noise of the external world and the chatter of our internal dialogues. Its benefits extend far beyond the meditation cushion, influencing every aspect of our lives. Integrating mindfulness into our daily routines can significantly enhance present-moment awareness, helping us to break free from the automatic pilot mode that often governs our actions and reactions. This heightened awareness brings richness to our experiences, allowing us to savour life's pleasures more fully and navigate its challenges with greater calm and resilience.

Moreover, mindfulness has been shown to play a crucial role in stress reduction. By fostering an attitude of acceptance and non-judgment, mindfulness practices help us to meet stress with equanimity, reducing its impact on our mental and physical health. This shift in perspective can transform our relationship with stress, enabling us to respond to pressures with clarity and balance rather than react from a place of overwhelm.

Integrating mindfulness into your day doesn't require extensive time commitments or special circumstances; rather, it's about finding opportunities within your existing routine to cultivate awareness and presence. Here are some practical tips and exercises to help make mindfulness an accessible and enriching part of your everyday life:

- **Mindful Breathing:** Start with the basics of mindful breathing. Take a few moments throughout your day to focus solely on your breath, noticing the sensation of air moving in and out of your body. This simple practice can serve as a calming anchor, bringing you back to the present moment whenever you feel scattered or stressed.

- **Mindful Eating:** Transform meals into mindfulness practices by eating slowly and with intention. Pay attention to the colours, textures, and flavours of your food, appreciating each bite. Mindful eating not only enhances the enjoyment of your meals but also promotes better digestion and satiety.

- **Incorporate Mindfulness into Daily Activities:** Find mindfulness in the mundane whether you're washing dishes, taking a shower, or walking to work. Engage fully with the experience, noticing the sensations and details of the activity.

This practice turns everyday tasks into opportunities for mindfulness.

- **Set Mindfulness Reminders:** In our busy lives, it's easy to forget to pause and be present. Setting reminders on your phone or computer can help cultivate a habit of taking short mindfulness breaks throughout the day, encouraging regular practice.

- **Mindfulness Apps and Resources:** Leverage technology to support your mindfulness journey. Numerous apps offer guided meditations, mindfulness exercises, and educational content to help integrate mindfulness into your life, regardless of your experience level.

As we embrace these practices, mindfulness becomes not just an exercise but a way of being, infusing our days with a sense of purpose and presence. This approach to life enriches our experiences, deepens our connections, and builds a resilient foundation for facing the complexities of the modern world.

Transitioning from the serene mindfulness practice, we move to the next pivotal aspect of our journey toward sustainable well-being: "The Power of Routine and Structure." In the following section, we'll explore how establishing a well-considered routine can create a framework for balance, productivity, and fulfilment, providing the stability and predictability we need to thrive in both our personal and professional lives.

The Power of Routine and Structure

At its core, a structured daily routine is about more than the predictability of what comes next; it's about establishing a rhythm that resonates with our deepest needs and aspirations. This rhythm provides a sense of stability in an often unpredictable world, grounding us amid the whirlwind of responsibilities and demands. By defining clear boundaries between work, leisure, and rest, we mitigate the overwhelm of decision fatigue, freeing our cognitive resources for creativity, problem-solving, and presence in the moment.

Decision fatigue, the deteriorating quality of decisions made after a long session of decision-making, can be a significant drain on our mental energy. A structured routine acts as a counterbalance to this fatigue, automating many of our daily decisions and preserving our mental bandwidth for those choices that truly matter. This automation creates a smoother, less stressful daily experience, allowing us to engage more fully with the task or moment at hand.

Crafting a routine that supports long-term well-being is both an art and a science. It requires a thoughtful consideration of our values, needs, and goals, balanced with the practicalities of our daily lives. Here are some strategies for creating routines that nourish and sustain:

- **Integration of Work and Leisure:** Balance is key. Ensure your routine includes blocks of focused work time, interspersed with periods of leisure and relaxation. This balance prevents burnout and keeps motivation and productivity high.

- **Prioritise Social Connection:** Humans are inherently social beings. Carve out time in your routine for connecting with friends, family, and community, whether it's a quick catch-up over coffee or a weekend gathering.

- **Self-care as a Non-negotiable:** Make self-care practices—be it mindfulness, exercise, or hobbies—a fixed part of your daily routine. These activities should be viewed not as luxuries, but as essential components of your day.

- **Flexibility and Personalisation:** While structure is important, so is flexibility. Life is unpredictable, and our routines must be adaptable. Personalise your routine to fit your lifestyle and be willing to adjust as circumstances change.

A routine that supports well-being is deeply personal. What works for one person may not work for another, underscoring the importance of personalisation in the development of your daily structure. Listen to your body and mind, and be prepared to iterate and evolve your routine as you discover what truly supports your well-being.

As we recognise the stabilising power of routine and structure in our lives, we also acknowledge the vital role of physical activity in sustaining our health and happiness. In the next chapter of this book, we will explore how incorporating regular movement into our routines can elevate our quality of life, enhance our mental state, and fortify us against the pressures of the modern world.

Physical Activity for Life

In the narrative of sustainable well-being, physical activity emerges not merely as a subplot but as a central theme—a dynamic force that enriches the storyline of our lives with vitality, resilience, and joy.

The benefits of regular physical activity extend far beyond the confines of physical health, touching every aspect of our well-being. Research consistently shows that exercise plays a significant role in enhancing mood, boosting energy levels, and reducing stress. For instance, studies published in renowned journals such as "The American Journal of Psychiatry" highlight the antidepressant effects of exercise, demonstrating its capacity to alleviate symptoms of depression and anxiety. Furthermore, physical activity has been shown to improve cognitive function, enhance sleep quality, and bolster our overall resilience to life's stressors.

Integrating physical activity into our daily lives doesn't require monumental changes or unwavering discipline. Instead, it's about finding joy and motivation in movement, transforming exercise from a chore into a cherished part of our day. Here are some suggestions for making physical activity a natural and enjoyable aspect of your routine:

- **Active Commuting:** Consider walking, cycling, or even roller-skating to work or while running errands. This incorporates exercise into your day while also connecting you with your surroundings and reducing your carbon footprint.

- **Recreational Sports and Activities:** Engage in sports or activities that spark joy, whether it's joining a local soccer team, taking dance classes, or hiking in nature. These activities offer the dual benefits of physical exercise and social interaction, enhancing your well-being on multiple levels.

- **Incorporate Movement Breaks:** Make a conscious effort to break up long periods of sitting with short movement breaks. A few minutes of stretching, stair climbing, or yoga can rejuvenate your body and mind, especially during busy workdays.

- **Family and Friend Fitness:** Involve family and friends in your physical activities. Whether it's a family bike ride, a friendly game of basketball, or a partner yoga session, sharing these experiences can deepen connections and make exercise more fun and rewarding.

- **Mindful Exercise:** Approach your physical activities with mindfulness, focusing on the sensations of movement and breath. This practice not only enhances the physical benefits of exercise but also fosters a deeper connection with your body and the present moment.

The connection between physical activity and mental health is well-documented, with numerous studies underscoring its importance. For example, research in "The Lancet Psychiatry" found a clear link between regular physical activity and reduced instances of depression, anxiety, and emotional distress. These studies reinforce the notion that movement is not just beneficial but essential for our mental and emotional health.

As we embrace physical activity as a vital component of our well-being, it becomes clear that the journey toward holistic health doesn't end here. The next chapter, "Nutrition for Mental Health," builds upon the foundation laid by physical activity, exploring how the foods we consume play an equally pivotal role in shaping our mental and emotional landscape. In this upcoming section, we'll delve into the synergy between diet and mental health, offering insights into how nutritional choices can support our journey toward sustainable well-being, complementing the physical vitality we cultivate through regular movement. Together, physical activity and nutrition form a powerful duo, each amplifying the benefits of the other, guiding us toward a life of balance, energy, and joy.

Nutrition for Mental Health

In the holistic journey toward sustainable well-being, the role of nutrition emerges as a pivotal chapter that is intricately linked to the narrative of mental health. As we navigate the complexities of modern living, understanding the impact of what we consume becomes a key to unlocking a life less susceptible to burnout and more vibrant with health and vitality.

The connection between the foods we eat and our mental health is profound and multifaceted. Nutritional psychiatry, an emerging field, underscores the significance of diet in influencing brain function and mood. Nutrients such as omega-3 fatty acids, antioxidants, vitamins, and minerals play critical roles in brain health, affecting neurotransmitter production, inflammation, and neural pathways. A diet rich in whole, nutrient-dense foods can uplift our mood, enhance cognitive function, and provide the energy we need to face life's challenges with resilience. Conversely, diets high in processed foods, sugar, and unhealthy fats can exacerbate symptoms of stress, anxiety, and depression, further contributing to the cycle of burnout.

Embracing a balanced diet that supports mental health doesn't require drastic changes or rigid restrictions. It's about making mindful choices that nourish both body and mind. Here are some guidelines to help cultivate a diet that champions mental well-being:

- **Whole Foods First:** Prioritise whole foods—fruits, vegetables, whole grains, lean proteins, and healthy fats. These foods provide a symphony of nutrients essential for brain health and overall vitality.

- **Omega-3 Rich Foods:** Incorporate sources of omega-3 fatty acids, such as fatty fish, flaxseeds, and walnuts, known for their anti-inflammatory properties and positive effects on mood and cognitive function.

- **Antioxidant-Rich Choices:** Load up on antioxidant-rich foods like berries, leafy greens, and nuts. Antioxidants combat oxidative stress, protecting brain cells and promoting mental clarity.

- **Mindful of Micronutrients:** Ensure a sufficient intake of vitamins and minerals, such as B vitamins, vitamin D, magnesium, and zinc, which play crucial roles in mood regulation and stress response.

- **Hydration and Herbal Teas:** Don't overlook the importance of hydration. Water is essential for optimal brain function, while herbal teas like chamomile and green tea offer calming and antioxidant benefits.

Creating meals that support mental health can be both simple and delicious. Here are a few ideas to inspire your culinary journey:

- **Breakfast:** Start the day with oatmeal topped with walnuts and berries, providing a blend of complex carbs, omega-3s, and antioxidants.

- **Lunch:** Opt for a quinoa salad with mixed greens, avocado, and grilled chicken or chickpeas, dressed in olive oil and lemon juice for a balanced mix of protein, healthy fats, and micronutrients.

- **Dinner:** Try baked salmon with a side of sweet potatoes and steamed broccoli—a meal rich in omega-3s, beta-carotene, and fibers.

- **Snacks:** Keep it simple with snacks like apple slices with almond butter or a small handful of mixed nuts.

By making conscious dietary choices, we can significantly influence our mental health and resilience against burnout. Nutrition is a powerful tool in our well-being arsenal - one that empowers us to nourish our bodies and minds from the inside out.

Prioritising Rest and Recovery

The prevention of burnout hinges significantly on our ability to prioritise rest and recovery within our daily lives. Quality sleep acts as the cornerstone of this foundation, providing the mental and physical repair our bodies demand after the day's exertions. Yet, rest encompasses more than sleep alone; it includes moments of relaxation, mindfulness, and leisure that allow our minds to wander, our bodies to rejuvenate, and our spirits to soar. In a world that often glorifies busyness, championing rest becomes a radical act of self-care and preservation.

To navigate the path toward improved sleep and restorative practices, consider the following strategies:

- **Cultivate a Sleep-Inducing Environment:** Create a bedroom oasis conducive to sleep—cool, dark, and quiet. Invest in comfortable bedding and consider white noise machines or blackout curtains to minimise disturbances.

- **Establish a Relaxing Pre-Sleep Routine:** Wind down each night with rituals that signal to your body it's time to rest. This might include reading, gentle stretching, or a warm bath. Avoid screens and stimulating activities that can disrupt your body's natural sleep rhythms.

- **Embrace Restorative Practices:** Incorporate practices like yoga, meditation, or deep-breathing exercises into your routine. These activities can reduce stress, calm the mind, and prepare the body for rest, enhancing overall sleep quality.

- **Listen to Your Body's Signals:** Become attuned to the signs that indicate a need for rest—fatigue, irritability, decreased concentration. Acknowledge these signals as legitimate requests for downtime, and respond with self-compassion by allowing yourself the rest you need.

- **Regularise Sleep Patterns:** Strive for consistency in your sleep schedule, going to bed, and waking up at the same times daily.

Regularity reinforces your body's sleep-wake cycle, improving sleep quality over time.

Listening to our bodies and minds is a skill cultivated with patience and attention. It requires us to tune into our internal experiences, recognising when fatigue is not merely a temporary nuisance but a signal that our reserves are depleted. By honouring these signals and prioritising rest, we not only prevent burnout but also embrace a lifestyle that values and nurtures our well-being.

As we conclude our exploration of Personal Habits for Long-term Balance, we've journeyed through the realms of mindfulness, routine, physical activity, nutrition, and rest. Each element plays a distinct yet interconnected role in weaving a tapestry of sustainable well-being. By adopting practices that enhance our presence, structure our days, energise our bodies, nourish our minds, and restore our spirits, we lay the groundwork for a life resilient against burnout and rich in fulfilment.

As we transition from the personal habits that fortify our individual well-being, we step into the broader landscape of "Corporate Responsibility." Here, we'll explore how the environments in which we work and the cultures we cultivate play a pivotal role in preventing burnout. This next chapter invites us to consider how organisations, leadership, and workplace policies can support or undermine our collective and individual journeys toward sustainable well-being.

CORPORATE RESPONSIBILITY

In the evolving landscape of workplace wellness, corporate responsibility stands as a pillar of burnout prevention and sustainable well-being. This chapter delves into how organisations can foster environments that mitigate the risk of burnout and also promote a culture of health, engagement, and productivity.

By focusing on creating a supportive culture, offering flexible work arrangements, providing mental and physical health support, and committing to regular assessments and improvements, businesses can play a pivotal role in preventing burnout and fostering an environment where employees not only survive but thrive.

Creating a Culture of Well-being

In the modern workplace, the cultivation of a culture that places well-being at its heart is not just a noble pursuit but a strategic imperative. This chapter delves into the profound significance of fostering a workplace culture where well-being is prioritised, showcasing the pivotal role leadership attitudes, company values, and the physical work environment play in shaping employee health and satisfaction. Through the lens of successful case studies, we'll explore the transformative strategies organisations have employed to weave well-being into the very fabric of their corporate culture, achieving remarkable outcomes in employee engagement, productivity, and overall job satisfaction.

The essence of a well-being-centric workplace culture lies in the recognition that employees are not just contributors to the bottom line but individuals with holistic needs that transcend the professional sphere.

Leadership attitudes and company values act as the compass guiding the organisation towards a culture of well-being. Leaders who model healthy work-life balance, openly discuss mental health and actively participate in well-being programs inspire employees to prioritise their own health. Company values that explicitly include well-being as a core principle reinforce this message, embedding it into the organisation's DNA and encouraging a collective commitment to nurturing a healthy workplace.

The physical work environment, too, plays a crucial role, with spaces designed for comfort, collaboration, and relaxation contributing significantly to employee well-being. The design and features of the physical work environment are tangible expressions of an organisation's commitment to well-being. Spaces that offer natural light, ergonomic workstations, quiet zones for relaxation, and areas for physical activity can dramatically enhance employee well-being. Additionally, creating communal spaces that encourage social interaction and connection fosters a sense of community and belonging, further supporting mental health and satisfaction.

Let's study these examples that showcase best practices and trends in corporate well-being observed in various industries:

- **Tech Innovators Inc.:** Tech Innovators Inc., a leading software development company, recognised the importance of mental health and work-life balance early on. They launched a "FlexTime" program, allowing employees to customise their working hours and location. Leadership also initiated regular "Mindful Mondays," where employees could participate in guided meditation sessions and workshops focused on stress management. Within a year, employee satisfaction surveys showed a 30% increase in work-life balance ratings and a 25% decrease in reported stress levels.

- **Global Manufacturing Solutions:** Global Manufacturing Solutions, a heavyweight in the manufacturing sector, addressed physical health head-on by introducing comprehensive wellness centres at their major facilities. These centres included state-of-the-art fitness equipment, on-site medical consultations, and spaces dedicated to relaxation and mindfulness practices. They also revamped their cafeteria menus to offer healthier, nutritionist-approved options. The impact was clear: a 20%

reduction in health-related absenteeism and a significant boost in employee energy levels and productivity.

- **Connective Consulting:** In the competitive world of consulting, Connective Consulting stood out by prioritising employee connection and community. They rolled out an "Everyone Connects" initiative, which included peer mentorship programs, quarterly team retreats focused on professional development and well-being, and open forums for employees to share their experiences and insights on balancing high work demands with personal well-being. The initiative not only improved employee morale but also led to a 15% decrease in employee turnover, with the firm being recognised in industry surveys as one of the best places to work for three consecutive years.

These case studies underscore the tangible benefits of integrating well-being into the corporate culture through thoughtful leadership, supportive policies, and environments that encourage health, connection, and balance. As we pivot to the concept of "Flexible Work Arrangements," we'll explore how the flexibility in when and where work is done further amplifies these benefits. In a world where the lines between work and life increasingly blur, finding harmony through flexibility becomes a key strategy in fostering a culture of sustainable well-being.

Flexible Work Arrangements

In an era where the boundaries between professional and personal life are increasingly blurred, the adoption of flexible work arrangements emerges as a transformative strategy for organisations aiming to foster a culture of well-being. By striking a balance that honours both organisational objectives and employee needs, companies can cultivate an environment that not only supports but thrives on flexibility, reducing stress, enhancing work-life balance, and boosting loyalty and productivity.

The introduction of flexible work arrangements represents a significant departure from traditional 9-to-5 work structures, offering a more personalised approach to work that acknowledges the individual needs of employees. The benefits of this flexibility are manifold:

- **Reduced Stress and Improved Work-Life Balance**: By allowing employees to adjust their work schedules or locations, organisations can significantly reduce the stress associated with rigid work hours and long commutes. This flexibility empowers employees to manage their work in harmony with personal responsibilities and preferences, leading to a healthier work-life balance.

- **Enhanced Employee Loyalty and Productivity**: Flexible work arrangements are often met with increased employee loyalty as workers feel valued and supported by their employers. This sense of trust and respect fosters a positive workplace culture which, in turn, boosts productivity. Employees are more motivated and engaged when they have control over their work schedules, leading to higher-quality output and innovation.

- **Attracting and Retaining Talent**: Offering flexibility in work arrangements positions a company as an attractive employer in competitive job markets. It signals a commitment to employee well-being and adaptability, qualities highly prized by today's workforce, particularly among younger generations who prioritise flexibility and work-life integration.

While the benefits are clear, implementing flexible work arrangements is not without its challenges. Organisations must navigate a series of considerations to ensure these practices align with business goals while meeting employee needs:

- **Maintaining Communication and Collaboration:** One of the primary challenges of telecommuting and flexible hours is ensuring consistent communication and collaboration among team members. Companies need to leverage technology and establish clear communication protocols to maintain team cohesion and workflow.

- **Setting Clear Expectations:** Clear guidelines regarding availability, work output, and deadlines are crucial in a flexible work environment. Both managers and employees should have a mutual understanding of expectations to prevent any confusion or misalignment.

- **Equity and Fairness:** Organisations must also consider how flexible work arrangements are offered and communicated to ensure fairness across the board. Policies should be applied equitably to prevent resentment or perceptions of favouritism among employees.

To effectively implement flexible work arrangements, organisations can adopt the following strategies:

- **Pilot Programs:** Before a full rollout, consider launching a pilot program to test the viability of flexible work arrangements. This approach allows for adjustments based on real-world feedback and experiences.

- **Training for Managers:** Equip managers with the tools and training needed to manage remote or flexibly scheduled teams effectively. Leadership development in these areas is crucial for navigating the unique challenges of flexible work environments.

- **Feedback Mechanisms:** Establish channels for ongoing feedback from employees participating in flexible work arrangements. This feedback is invaluable for refining policies and practices to better suit both employee and organisational needs.

As we explore the landscape of flexible work arrangements, it's evident that when thoughtfully implemented, these practices can significantly contribute to a culture of well-being within the workplace. In an environment that values flexibility and work-life balance, prioritising mental health becomes a natural extension of the organisation's commitment to its employees' overall well-being. Together, these strategies form a comprehensive approach to creating a workplace that not only adapts to the changing dynamics of the modern world but also actively supports and nurtures the health and happiness of its workforce.

Supporting Mental Health in the Workplace

In the contemporary workplace, the conversation around mental health has transitioned from a whispered taboo to a central focus of corporate wellness initiatives. This shift recognises a fundamental truth: the mental health of employees is not just a personal issue but a critical factor influencing organisational health, productivity, and culture.

The need for mental health support in corporate environments cannot be overstated. With the increasing pressures of the modern work landscape, employees often face challenges that can lead to stress, anxiety, and other mental health issues, affecting their performance, engagement, and overall quality of life. Recognising and addressing these challenges through structured support systems is not just an act of compassion; it's a strategic imperative that benefits the entire organisation.

Several key initiatives have proven effective in supporting mental health in the workplace:

- **Employee Assistance Programs (EAPs):** EAPs offer confidential counselling services to employees dealing with personal or work-related issues. By providing access to professional mental health support, EAPs serve as a critical resource, helping employees navigate life's challenges while maintaining their focus and productivity at work.

- **Mental Health Days:** Recognising the importance of mental rest and recovery, some organisations have begun to offer mental health days—paid leave that employees can use to recharge and address their mental health needs. This initiative supports employee well-being and also signals organisational recognition of mental health as a priority, on par with physical health.

- **Managerial Training:** Equipping managers with the skills to recognise and respond to signs of mental distress among team members is crucial. Training programs can provide managers the tools to approach sensitive conversations, offer support, and guide employees toward available resources, fostering a culture of openness and care.

Research and statistics offer compelling evidence of the positive impact of mental health initiatives on both organisational and individual levels. Studies have shown that companies investing in mental health support report lower absenteeism rates, higher employee satisfaction, and improved productivity. For instance, a report by the World Health Organisation found that for every dollar invested in scaling up treatment for common mental disorders, there is a return of four dollars in improved health and productivity.

Moreover, organisations that prioritise mental health often see enhanced employee loyalty and a stronger employer brand, attracting talent in increasingly competitive markets. These benefits underscore the value of mental health support not just as a moral obligation but as a strategic advantage.

As we underscore the importance of supporting mental health in the workplace, we also recognise that well-being extends beyond the psychological realm. The next chapter, "Encouraging Physical Activity and Nutritional Health," will explore how organisations can promote holistic health by fostering environments that encourage physical wellness. From on-site fitness facilities to wellness challenges and nutritional education, we'll delve into strategies that support the physical health of employees as a complement to mental health initiatives.

Encouraging Physical Activity and Nutritional Health

In the comprehensive journey toward fostering a culture of well-being within the corporate sphere, the promotion of physical health stands out as a critical chapter. This section of our narrative delves into the multifaceted role organisations play in nurturing the physical wellness of their employees. By providing on-site fitness facilities, encouraging participation in sports and recreational events, and promoting nutritional health through various initiatives, businesses can significantly contribute to a healthier, more vibrant workforce.

The modern workplace has evolved to recognise that employee well-being extends far beyond mere job satisfaction or financial compensation. Physical health, an indispensable component of overall well-being, is increasingly becoming a focus of corporate wellness programs. Here's how organisations are stepping up to the challenge:

- **On-Site Fitness Facilities:** Providing employees with convenient access to fitness centres, gyms, or even simple workout areas within the office can dramatically increase the likelihood of regular physical activity. These facilities offer a practical solution for employees to incorporate exercise into their daily routines, effectively breaking down one of the most significant barriers to regular physical activity: time constraints.

- **Organised Sport and Recreation Events:** Hosting company-wide sports events, fitness challenges, or recreational activities not only encourages physical activity but also fosters team spirit and camaraderie among employees. Whether it's a corporate marathon, a weekly yoga class, or a company sports league, these initiatives provide fun and engaging ways for employees to stay active.

- **Incentives for Active Commuting:** Encouraging employees to walk, cycle, or run to work by providing incentives such as bike racks, showers, and locker facilities, or even financial incentives, can promote a more active commute. These practices not only contribute to physical health but also to environmental sustainability.

Nutrition plays a pivotal role in maintaining energy levels, concentration, and overall health. Organisations have a unique opportunity to influence the dietary habits of their employees positively in such ways:

- **Healthy Eating Options in Cafeterias:** By offering a variety of healthy, appealing food options in company cafeterias, organisations can make it easier for employees to make nutritious choices. Collaborating with dietitians or nutritionists to design balanced meal options can ensure that employees have access to meals that support their well-being.

- **Nutritional Workshops and Education:** Hosting workshops or seminars on topics related to nutrition, healthy eating habits, and meal planning can empower employees with the knowledge to make informed dietary choices. These educational initiatives can cover a range of topics, from the basics of nutrition to how to read food labels and prepare healthy meals at home.

- **Access to Fresh, Healthy Snacks:** Replacing traditional vending machine fare with fresh fruit, nuts, and other healthy snack options can make a significant difference in employees' daily eating habits. Making these healthier options readily available encourages employees to snack smartly during their workday.

As organisations invest in promoting physical activity and nutritional health, it's crucial to recognise that these initiatives are not static. The evolving needs of the workforce and the dynamic nature of wellness itself necessitate a commitment to regular assessments and continuous improvement. The next chapter, "Regular Assessments and Continuous Improvement," delves into the strategies for evaluating the effectiveness of health and wellness programs, gathering feedback from employees, and making data-driven adjustments to enhance these initiatives over time. Through this iterative process, organisations can fine-tune their approach to employee well-being, ensuring that their efforts remain aligned with the goal of fostering a healthy, productive, and satisfied workforce.

Regular Assessments and Continuous Improvement

In the quest for a healthier, more resilient workforce, the journey doesn't end with the implementation of well-being initiatives. The true path to sustainable change lies in the cycle of regular assessments and continuous improvement. This critical chapter of our narrative emphasises the importance of evaluating workplace well-being programs, ensuring they not only meet current needs but also adapt to the evolving landscape of employee health and satisfaction.

Regular assessments serve as the compass that guide the direction of well-being initiatives, providing invaluable insights into their effectiveness and areas for enhancement. Surveys, for instance, offer a direct line to employee perceptions and experiences, shedding light on the impact of current programs and unmet needs. Feedback mechanisms (such as suggestion boxes or digital platforms) encourage ongoing dialogue between employees and management, fostering a culture of openness and collaboration. Health and wellness audits, conducted periodically, evaluate the comprehensiveness of wellness offerings, ensuring they align with best practices and industry standards.

The **feedback** gathered through these assessments is the bedrock upon which continuous improvement is built. It enables organisations to identify successful elements of their well-being programs as well as those requiring adjustment. This iterative process ensures that initiatives remain relevant and responsive to the changing dynamics of the workforce. By engaging employees in the evaluation process, organisations can cultivate a sense of ownership and investment in the well-being program.

A cornerstone of effective well-being programs is the **establishment of clear, measurable goals**. These objectives should be SMART: Specific, Measurable, Achievable, Relevant, and Time-bound. Goals might range from reducing absenteeism rates to improving scores on employee satisfaction surveys or increasing participation in wellness activities. By defining these targets, organisations can create a roadmap for success, focusing efforts and resources on achieving tangible outcomes.

Tracking progress toward these goals is essential for maintaining momentum and engagement in well-being initiatives. Employing tools such as wellness dashboards or regular progress reports can provide both leadership and employees with a clear view of advancements. Celebrating successes, big or small, plays a crucial role in sustaining enthusiasm and commitment to the program. Recognising individual or team achievements, sharing success stories, and marking milestones can reinforce the value of the well-being program, encouraging continued participation and effort.

As we conclude our exploration of "Corporate Responsibility" in the landscape of prevention and sustainable well-being, it's clear that organisations play a pivotal role in shaping the health and happiness of their workforce. From creating cultures that prioritise well-being and offering flexible work arrangements to supporting mental health and promoting physical health, businesses have the opportunity to lead by example. The commitment to regular assessments and continuous improvement ensures that these efforts not only meet the immediate needs of employees but also adapt and evolve over time. In doing so, organisations can build a legacy of well-being, crafting workplaces that are not just productive but truly thriving environments where every employee has the opportunity to achieve their best health and well-being.

As we move forward, the journey of fostering a supportive, healthy workplace continues to unfold, reminding us that well-being is a dynamic, ongoing process. The lessons learned and strategies developed in this chapter serve as a foundation for future efforts, guiding us toward a world where well-being in the workplace is not an aspiration but a reality.

BUILDING A SUPPORTIVE COMMUNITY

In the final leg of our journey through "Prevention and Sustainable Well-Being," let's turn our attention to the power of community. This subsection explores how building supportive networks (both within and outside the workplace) can bolster individual resilience, foster a sense of belonging, and contribute to overall mental health and happiness.

The Role of Community in Well-Being

In the tapestry of our lives, the threads that bind us to others—our communities—play a pivotal role in weaving patterns of well-being, resilience, and fulfilment. "The Role of Community in Well-Being," a crucial chapter in our exploration of prevention and sustainable well-being, delves into the profound psychological and emotional benefits of being part of a supportive network.

Belonging to a supportive community offers a sanctuary of understanding, empathy, and shared experiences. The psychological benefits of such connections are profound: they instil a sense of security and acceptance which are vital components in the foundation of our mental well-being. Emotionally, these connections fulfil our inherent need for belonging, a primal urge that, when satisfied, can elevate our happiness and satisfaction with life. Communities—be they formed by family, friends, colleagues, or shared interest groups—act as a mirror reflecting our value and place in the world, reinforcing our sense of identity and self-worth.

Social connections offer more than just emotional comfort; they provide a tangible buffer against the pressures and stresses of life. The support we receive from our community—whether through a listening ear, shared advice, or simply the presence of others—can significantly mitigate the impact of stress. This support system acts as a shock absorber, cushioning us from the jolts of personal and professional challenges and enabling us to navigate life's ups and downs with greater resilience.

The link between strong social networks and mental health is well-documented in scientific literature. Research consistently shows that individuals with robust social connections have a lower incidence of mental health challenges including depression and anxiety. A study published in the "American Journal of Psychiatry" highlights how social support significantly lowers the risk of developing major depressive disorder, illustrating the protective role of social ties.

Furthermore, the benefits of a supportive community extend to the realm of burnout prevention. The "Journal of Occupational Health Psychology" has published findings indicating that strong workplace social networks can reduce the risk of burnout among employees by providing emotional support and facilitating coping mechanisms that buffer against work-related stress.

The longevity and quality of our lives are also influenced by the strength of our social connections. Research in the "Journal of Health and Social Behaviour" suggests that individuals with strong social ties tend to live longer, healthier lives, attributing this to the positive impact of community on behaviours and attitudes that contribute to physical health alongside the direct stress-buffering effects of social support.

As we reflect on the integral role of community in our well-being, it becomes evident that the support, belonging, and connection we derive from our social networks are indispensable elements of a fulfilling life. These insights not only highlight the necessity of nurturing our personal and professional relationships but also lay the groundwork for the next critical aspect of building sustainable well-being: "Creating Supportive Work Environments."

The principles underpinning supportive communities can and should be mirrored within our workplaces. By fostering environments that encourage connection, empathy, and mutual support, organisations can amplify the benefits of community, extending the reach of well-being initiatives to touch every aspect of an employee's life. This holistic approach to well-being recognises that the health of an organisation is intrinsically linked to the health of its members, underscoring the imperative for workplaces to be spaces of productivity and sanctuaries of support and belonging.

Creating Supportive Work Environments

Creating supportive work environments where community and connection flourish is not just a matter of corporate responsibility; it's a strategic investment in the heart of an organisation—its people. This chapter unfolds the numerous ways in which organisations can cultivate a sense of community among employees, transforming the workplace into a hub of engagement, support, and mutual respect. Through team-building activities, shared wellness challenges, and thoughtfully designed spaces for social interaction, businesses can foster an atmosphere where employees feel genuinely connected and valued.

One of the most effective strategies for nurturing community within the workplace is the implementation of **team-building activities**. These activities, ranging from problem-solving challenges to creative workshops, encourage collaboration and deepen interpersonal relationships among team members. When employees engage in tasks outside the usual scope of work, they discover new facets of their colleagues' personalities, fostering empathy and understanding that bridge professional roles and hierarchies.

Shared wellness challenges (such as fitness competitions or mindfulness months) unite employees towards common health goals, creating a collective journey towards well-being. These challenges not only promote healthy habits but also spark conversations about well-being, making wellness a shared value within the organisation.

Physical spaces dedicated to social interaction play a pivotal role in facilitating community. Break rooms, communal dining areas, and outdoor spaces designed for relaxation and conversation can significantly enhance social cohesion. These spaces invite spontaneous interactions and provide settings where employees can share personal stories, celebrate successes, and offer support during challenging times, reinforcing a sense of belonging.

Here's how successful community-building initiatives might look like:

- **GreenTech Innovations**: GreenTech Innovations launched a "Healthy Habits" challenge, encouraging teams to track their daily water intake, steps, and mindfulness practices. The challenge was supported by an app where employees could share progress, tips, and words of encouragement. This initiative not only improved physical well-being but also fostered a supportive network of colleagues invested in each other's health. Post-challenge surveys reported a 40% increase in team cohesion and a significant boost in overall job satisfaction.

- **Creative Solutions Agency**: At Creative Solutions Agency, the introduction of "Idea Lounges"—spaces designed for relaxation and casual brainstorming—transformed the company culture. These lounges became the birthplace of innovative projects, facilitated by the free exchange of ideas in a relaxed setting. The initiative led to a surge in creative collaboration and a deeper sense of community with employees reporting feeling more valued and inspired.

- **Global Finance Corp**: Recognising the importance of mental health, Global Finance Corp instituted monthly "Wellness Workshops" led by experts in nutrition, stress management, and financial well-being. These workshops provided a platform for employees to learn, discuss, and apply new well-being strategies, fostering a culture where personal growth and support were paramount. Following the workshops, employee engagement scores rose by 30%, highlighting the effectiveness of educational initiatives in building community.

The strategies and successes highlighted in this chapter underscore the profound impact of creating supportive work environments on employee well-being and organisational health. By prioritising community through team-building, wellness initiatives, and social spaces, organisations can cultivate an atmosphere where employees thrive together.

The next chapter, "Leveraging Technology to Build Connections," explores how digital tools and platforms can enhance the sense of community among employees, bridging distances and schedules to create a cohesive, engaged workforce. In this digital age, technology holds the potential to transform the way we connect, collaborate, and care for one another within the workplace, propelling us towards a future where community and technology converge to support well-being in new and innovative ways.

Leveraging Technology to Build Connections

In an era where digital technology permeates every aspect of our lives, its role in shaping workplace connections and community cannot be overlooked. This chapter explores the dual-edged nature of digital platforms and social media in the workplace—how they can be harnessed to foster meaningful relationships and support networks, particularly for remote workers and geographically dispersed teams, while also emphasising the critical need for digital well-being and appropriate boundaries.

The advent of digital platforms has revolutionised the way we connect, making it possible to maintain and strengthen relationships across distances that would have once seemed insurmountable. For remote workers and teams spread across different locations, these platforms offer a lifeline, a way to feel connected to the broader organisational community. Video conferencing tools, instant messaging apps, and collaborative online workspaces enable real-time collaboration, mimicking the immediacy of in-person interactions. Social media and internal company networks provide spaces for employees to share successes, challenges, and moments from their personal lives, fostering a sense of belonging and camaraderie.

These digital tools have the potential to create a virtual support network, where employees can access advice, encouragement, and a sense of shared experience, regardless of physical location. This virtual community can be particularly beneficial in times of stress or isolation, offering a reminder that no one is alone in their challenges.

As much as digital platforms can enhance connectivity, they also raise concerns about digital well-being. The constant connectivity afforded by technology can blur the boundaries between work and personal life, leading to digital overload and burnout. Hence, setting boundaries around technology use is paramount to ensure that it serves to enhance rather than detract from social connections and overall well-being.

Organisations can play a crucial role in promoting digital well-being by encouraging employees to disconnect outside work hours, respecting digital boundaries and providing training on managing digital communication effectively. Creating "tech-free" times or spaces can help employees take necessary breaks from digital stimuli, promoting mental rest and recovery. Encouraging mindful use of technology—being intentional about when and how digital tools are used—can help mitigate the risk of digital fatigue and ensure that technology remains a tool for positive connection.

Encouraging healthy digital interaction involves creating policies that respect personal time such as limiting after-hours communication and setting expectations for response times. It also means fostering an online culture that values quality of interactions over quantity where digital communication is purposeful and meaningful rather than overwhelming.

Training and resources can equip employees with strategies to manage their digital interactions such as using "do not disturb" features during focused work times or personal hours, prioritising tasks to manage email and message overload, and using digital tools that facilitate rather than complicate communication.

Leveraging technology to build connections offers a gateway to a more inclusive, supportive, and connected workplace, bridging distances and creating a virtual space where community thrives. As we harness these digital tools for positive connection, we also pave the way for broader engagement with the community beyond the digital realm.

Transitioning from the virtual to the tangible, the next chapter, "Community Involvement and Volunteering," explores how organisations and individuals can extend the spirit of community and connection into direct action and engagement. This move from digital platforms to hands-on involvement not only deepens the sense of purpose and belonging among employees but also reinforces the organisation's commitment to societal well-being.

Community Involvement and Volunteering

In the rich mosaic of strategies designed to foster sustainable well-being, community involvement and volunteering stand out as vibrant pieces that encapsulate the profound impact of reaching beyond the confines of our immediate environments to touch the broader community. This chapter explores the numerous benefits of engaging in volunteering and civic involvement, not only as avenues for personal growth and fulfilment but also as essential components of a holistic approach to well-being.

Engaging with the community through volunteering offers a unique blend of benefits, fostering a sense of connection, purpose, and fulfilment that transcends the act of giving itself. The experience of contributing to the greater good, of making a tangible difference in the lives of others, ignites a deep sense of satisfaction and meaning. This outward expression of empathy and compassion not only enriches the lives of recipients but also bolsters the mental and emotional well-being of the volunteer, creating a cycle of positive impact.

The research underscores the psychological benefits of volunteering, linking it to lower levels of depression, increased life satisfaction, and a heightened sense of belonging. Moreover, civic involvement offers a platform for skill development and personal growth, presenting opportunities to tackle new challenges, foster leadership abilities, and build resilience.

Organisations play a pivotal role in promoting community involvement, offering a bridge between individual employees and larger societal needs. Here are examples of how businesses can foster a culture of volunteering:

- **Volunteer Time Off (VTO) Policies:** Some companies have instituted VTO policies, granting employees paid leave to engage in volunteer work. This not only underscores the organisation's commitment to community service but also empowers employees to contribute to causes they are passionate about without financial or time constraints.

- **Corporate Volunteer Programs:** By partnering with local charities, NGOs, or community projects, companies can create structured volunteer programs that align with their corporate values and areas of expertise. These programs can range from environmental clean-ups to mentoring youth, offering diverse opportunities for employee involvement.

- **Matching Gifts and Grants:** Encouraging charitable giving through matching gifts amplifies the impact of individual donations, while community grants for projects proposed by employees can foster a sense of ownership and pride in their contributions to societal well-being.

The mutual benefits of community involvement are evident. For employees, volunteering provides a sense of achievement, enhances well-being, and offers opportunities for social connection and skill development. For communities, the infusion of volunteer effort and corporate resources can make a significant difference in addressing local challenges and improving quality of life.

Here's how successful volunteering initiatives might look like:

- **Green Horizons Initiative:** Green Horizons Initiative, a mid-sized tech company, launched a community garden project in collaboration with a local environmental group. Employees volunteered to transform vacant city lots into thriving community gardens. The project beautified neighbourhoods and provided fresh produce to local residents while also fostering team cohesion and employee pride in contributing to sustainable urban development.

- **Mentorship Matters Program:** Mentorship Matters, a program initiated by a national insurance firm, paired employees with students from underprivileged backgrounds for one-on-one mentoring. The program aimed to inspire students to pursue higher education and careers in finance. For employees, the experience of mentoring provided profound personal growth and a deeper connection to the community, reinforcing the company's commitment to social responsibility.

As we reflect on the undeniable benefits of community involvement and volunteering, it becomes clear that these activities extend far beyond mere acts of charity. As we transition from the collective impact of community service to the personal sphere, our focus shifts to "Nurturing Personal Networks." This next chapter explores the importance of cultivating and maintaining personal relationships that support and enrich our lives, highlighting how the principles of empathy, connection, and support that underpin successful community engagement are equally essential in the realm of our personal interactions.

Nurturing Personal Networks

This chapter delves into the nuanced dance of cultivating and maintaining personal relationships that fortify our well-being, offering practical advice on effective communication, the establishment of healthy boundaries, and the cultivation of mutual support.

The foundation of any enduring personal network is the quality of its relationships. To cultivate and maintain connections that truly support well-being, consider the following strategies:

- **Effective Communication:** At the heart of all healthy relationships lies effective communication. This encompasses not only the ability to express oneself clearly and openly but also the capacity to listen deeply and empathetically. Cultivating these skills enables us to share our experiences, needs, and support more fully, fostering understanding and closeness.

- **Setting Healthy Boundaries:** Equally important is the establishment of healthy boundaries. These boundaries define the limits of what we find acceptable and unacceptable in our interactions with others. They are essential for maintaining our well-being. They allow us to protect our energy and emotional health, enabling us to engage in relationships in a way that is respectful to both ourselves and others.

- **Mutual Support:** The essence of a supportive network is reciprocity—relationships where support flows both ways. Cultivating a culture of mutual support within personal networks means being there for others just as they are there for you, sharing in both the joys and the challenges that life presents. This mutual support becomes a wellspring of strength and resilience for all involved.

Beyond the mechanics of communication and boundaries lies the broader landscape of our social networks, rich with potential for growth and enrichment. Embracing diversity within these networks encourages us to seek out and nurture connections with individuals from different backgrounds, cultures, and life experiences. These diverse connections challenge us to see the world from new perspectives, inspire us with fresh ideas, and enrich our understanding of the complex tapestry of human experience.

Diverse networks also expose us to a variety of coping strategies and viewpoints, enhancing our ability to navigate life's challenges and broadening our capacity for empathy and compassion. By actively seeking connections that stretch us, we not only enhance our personal well-being but also contribute to a more inclusive, understanding, and connected world.

Nurturing personal networks rich in effective communication, healthy boundaries, mutual support, and diversity is an ongoing journey that demands mindfulness, effort, and openness. Yet, the rewards of this journey are immeasurable, offering us a foundation of support, understanding, and connection that not only sustains us through life's challenges but also amplifies its joys.

As we close this chapter on "Nurturing Personal Networks," we are reminded of the profound impact our relationships have on our well-being. These connections, carefully cultivated and maintained, become our sanctuary, our sounding board, and our celebration squad. They remind us of our shared humanity, interconnectedness, and capacity to both give and receive support. In nurturing these networks, we not only enhance our own lives but also contribute to the well-being of our communities, weaving threads of connection that strengthen the fabric of society itself.

Concluding our exploration of "Building a Supportive Community," we're reminded of the fundamental human need for connection and the profound impact that fulfilling this need has on our well-being. The strategies and insights shared in this chapter illuminate the various pathways through which individuals and organisations can cultivate environments where supportive communities thrive. By prioritising the creation and maintenance of these networks, we lay the groundwork for a culture of well-being that extends beyond the individual, enveloping workplaces, families, and the broader community in a shared commitment to health, happiness, and resilience.

In embracing the principles outlined in this chapter, we are equipped to not only prevent burnout but to elevate our collective experience of well-being, forging connections that sustain us through challenges and enrich our lives with meaning and joy. This understanding propels us forward, ready to engage with the world in ways that foster well-being for ourselves and those around us, marking a fitting transition to our concluding reflections on the journey of prevention and sustainable well-being.

Conclusion

As we draw the curtains on Part Three of our exploration of "Burnout Prevention" and "Sustainable Well-Being," we find ourselves standing at the threshold of a transformed perspective on health, happiness, and holistic living. Throughout this journey, we've traversed the landscapes of personal habits, corporate responsibility, and the invaluable role of community, unearthing insights and strategies that pave the way for a life less susceptible to burnout and more vibrant with fulfilment.

This journey has illuminated the profound truth that well-being is not a destination but a continuous voyage—a delicate balance of nurturing the mind, body, and spirit in harmony with those around us. From the personal practices that ground us in mindfulness and physical vitality to the organisational cultures that support our growth and resilience and the communities that connect us to a larger purpose, each chapter has added layers to our understanding of what it means to live well.

We've seen how individual actions, like adopting mindful habits, engaging in regular physical activity, and prioritising nutrition and rest, form the bedrock of our personal well-being. Yet, these practices do not exist in isolation. They are profoundly influenced by the environments in which we work and live—environments that organisations have the power to shape. Through initiatives that foster supportive workspaces, encourage flexibility and champion mental health, businesses can create ecosystems where well-being flourishes.

Moreover, the journey has underscored the indispensable role of community in our lives. In a world that often feels fragmented, building and nurturing connections—whether through digital platforms, volunteering, or simply investing in our personal networks—emerges as a vital source of strength, support, and joy. These connections remind us that we are not alone, that our well-being is intrinsically linked to the well-being of others, and that together, we can create ripples of positive change that extend far beyond our immediate circles.

As we conclude this book, it's clear that the path to burnout prevention and sustainable well-being is multifaceted, requiring a holistic approach that integrates personal practices, organisational support, and community engagement. It's a path that asks us to be mindful of our choices, compassionate in our interactions, and intentional in our actions. It challenges us to look beyond the surface of well-being as merely the absence of illness, seeing it instead as an opportunity to cultivate a life rich in meaning, connection, and joy.

The journey toward burnout prevention and sustainable well-being is an ongoing, ever-evolving process of learning, adapting, and growing. It invites us to be architects of our own well-being and to engage actively in shaping the environments and relationships that define our lives. This journey challenges us to look beyond the immediate and to envision a life marked by balance, resilience, and deep fulfilment in order to take deliberate steps toward realising that vision.

In closing, let us reflect on the words of philosopher and poet John O'Donohue, who reminds us that "It is in the shelter of each other that the people live." May we find shelter in the communities we create, the connections we nurture, and the collective efforts we undertake to foster a world where well-being is not just an individual aspiration but a shared reality. Together, let us step forward into a future where prevention and sustainable well-being are woven into the very essence of our lives and our societies, creating a legacy of health, happiness, and wholeness for generations to come.

WHILE CREATING THIS BOOK, THE FOLLOWING RESOURCES WERE USED:

1. Aronsson, G., Theorell, T., Grape, T., Hammarström, A., Hogstedt, C., Marteinsdottir, I., Skoog, I., Träskman-Bendz, L., & Hall, C. (2017). "A systematic review including meta-analysis of work environment and burnout symptoms." *BMC Public Health.*

2. Demerouti, E., Bakker, A. B., Nachreiner, F., & Schaufeli, W. B. (2001). "The job demands-resources model of burnout." *Journal of Applied Psychology.*

3. Freudenberger, H. J. (1974). "Staff burn-out." *Journal of Social Issues.*

4. Goleman, D., Boyatzis, R., & McKee, A. (2002). *Primal Leadership: Learning to Lead with Emotional Intelligence.* Harvard Business School Press.

5. Lazarus, R. S., & Folkman, S. (1984). *Stress, Appraisal, and Coping.* Springer Publishing Company.

6. Maslach, C., & Leiter, M. P. (2016). "Understanding the burnout experience: Recent research and its implications for psychiatry." *The World Psychiatry Journal.*

7. Petersen, A., & Morgan, K. (2018). "Managing and mitigating fatigue in the workplace." *Occupational Medicine.*

8. Schaufeli, W. B., & Bakker, A. B. (2004). "Job demands-resources theory: Taking stock and looking forward." *Journal of Occupational Health Psychology.*

9. Siegrist, J. (1996). "Adverse health effects of high-effort/low-reward conditions." *Journal of Occupational Health Psychology.*

10. World Health Organization. (2019). *International Classification of Diseases, 11th Revision (ICD-11)*. WHO.

11. American Psychological Association. "Stress in America™ Survey." 2020.

12. Goleman, Daniel. *Emotional Intelligence: Why It Can Matter More Than IQ*. Bantam Books, 1995.

13. Kabat-Zinn, Jon. *Full Catastrophe Living: Using the Wisdom of Your Body and Mind to Face Stress, Pain, and Illness*. Delta, 1990.

14. Peer, Marisa. *Rapid Transformational Therapy: A Guided Process for Healing and Empowerment*. Self-published, 2017.

JOIN THE JOURNEY BEYOND THE BOOK

Thank you for turning the final page of "Burn In: The Ultimate Guide to Burnout Recovery and Prevention." If you found the strategies and insights within these pages enlightening, the journey doesn't have to end here.

WHO I AM AND HOW I CAN HELP FURTHER

I'm Valeria Savenko, a hypnosis expert specialising in stress management, confidence boosting, and helping individuals like you achieve financial freedom. My career began after a profound personal transformation through hypnosis helped me recover from career-threatening burnout not once but twice. Today, I dedicate my expertise to empowering others to lead stress-free and prosperous lives.

TAKE THE NEXT STEP WITH ME

I invite you to join our vibrant Facebook community, "Worry Less Earn More." This exclusive group is a sanctuary where like-minded individuals gather to share, learn, and grow. Here's what you can expect:

- **Ongoing Support:** Continue your journey of personal and professional growth with the support of a community that cares.

- **Exclusive Content:** Access new strategies, live sessions, and the latest insights that I only share in this group.

- **Real Connections:** Meet others who are on the same path and build relationships that inspire and support.

WHY JOIN NOW?

Don't let another day pass feeling overwhelmed by stress or uncertainty about your financial future. Joining "Worry Less Earn More" is your next step towards a life where peace and prosperity are the norm, not the exception. Plus, for a limited time, new members will receive an exclusive welcome packet with resources that complement your journey through "Burn In."

EASY TO JOIN!

Getting involved is simple. Just click the link below, and you'll be directed to the Facebook group where you can request to join. We can't wait to welcome you into our community!

Join the Worry Less Earn More Facebook Group Now!

Scan me!

Your new chapter begins today—make it count. Dive deeper, connect with peers, and continue building the life you deserve. Remember, empowerment is just a click away. See you there!

With gratitude,
Valeria Savenko

ABOUT THE AUTHOR

Valeria Savenko is a renowned expert in hypnosis and rapid mindset transformation with a sharp focus on stress management, anxiety relief, and confidence boosting. Her career in therapy and consulting took off in 2021 after she experienced profound burnout in her IT job. Seeking a swift recovery, Valeria discovered the powerful impact of hypnosis, not just for herself but as a life-changing tool for others.

Today, when Valeria isn't sailing the world, she's passionately helping seasoned entrepreneurs boost their wealth and gain financial freedom while working less than they ever did before. She tackles money-related anxiety and shatters financial mental blocks using her deep understanding of hypnosis, NLP, and mindset transformation coaching.

Want to know more about how Valeria Savenko can help you live a less stressed and wealthier life? Dive into her "Less Stress, More Wealth" Facebook group today and start transforming your life with her expert guidance!

www.ingramcontent.com/pod-product-compliance
Lightning Source LLC
Chambersburg PA
CBHW071020120626
46546CB00003B/1176